THE PUZZLE OF ARCHITECTURE

BY THE SAME AUTHOR

Victorian Modern

Australia's Home

The Australian Ugliness

The Walls Around Us

Kenzo Tange

The Puzzle of Architecture

ROBIN BOYD

MELBOURNE UNIVERSITY PRESS

LONDON AND NEW YORK: CAMBRIDGE UNIVERSITY PRESS

First published 1965

Printed and bound in Australia by
Melbourne University Press, Carlton N.3, Victoria

Registered in Australia for transmission
by post as a book

Dewey Decimal Classification Number 724.9
Library of Congress Catalog Card Number 65-25314

Text set in 10 point Grotesque Medium type

For D.P.B.

CONTENTS

INTRODUCTION

My early years in architecture were spent in an atmosphere of conflict in the middle of the greatest revolution in architectural history. The established order was represented by stale grey copies of buildings designed long dark centuries ago. The challenger represented all purity and light and progress and eternal goodness in design. We called it modern architecture. This was in Melbourne in the mid-1930s and the revolution was a thin reflection, after nearly ten years, of the original one in Europe. It was also of a slightly different character. In Europe the opposing sides were clearly black or white. Here there were several shades of grey.

The architectural profession was about equally divided on ideological grounds, split into two largely on an age grouping. Half the offices, the older ones, were determined to stick to their styles and honestly believed even then that 'Modern' was a nasty stunt that would go away soon if they did not look at it. The other architectural offices were more inclined by temperament to the new thing. Most of these also treated Modern rather as a fashionable stunt, but unlike the conservatives they approved the stunt. There was a thin aura of prestige of bravery attached to anyone who, as they said, 'went Modern'. Thus they added Modern to the alternative styles which they discussed with their clients, and if the client looked really daring sometimes they even suggested the Modern before the Georgian. Only very rarely was the client actually so daring as to accept, but when such a one did come along he was known as a good client. All the rest were known as bad clients. Despite the great number of bad clients about at that time, there were a few architects who had nothing but good clients. These were regarded with some awe, bewilderment and resentment. Why should anyone have all the luck? But these were the architects who understood what the battle was about.

1

The anonymous glass box

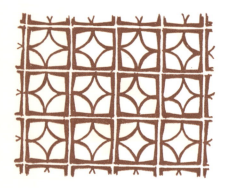

Edward Durrell Stone's grille

The issues really could be stated very simply and clearly. Modern architecture was attacking the old rule of the historical styles. It was also attacking the rules of composition: the concepts of proportion, symmetry, and so on. It was also attacking ornament. Ornament in fact was the symbol of the old that first had to be torn down by the new. Modern architecture then was campaigning on a straightforward and uncomplicated principle. It was rational, clean, uncluttered. No dust traps. It was universal —hence an 'International Style'. It was true, and as pure white as the paint on its plastered walls. It was as honest and open as the big windows sliced into the walls.

Everyone knows who won that fight, although no one actually saw it happen. The old styles were vanquished somehow off-stage when we were all looking the other way during World War II. When building started again in quantity about 1950 the International Style was undisputed victor and a pure anonymous glass box was the shining, attainable goal for every building. But not for long. Almost immediately critics began to question internationalism in building and denounce its extreme simplicity and to call for a return to more warm, human, togetherness qualities. Then engineers who had been working quietly in a back room came out with some exciting shapes in solid geometry. Then Edward Stone discovered the grille, and Le Corbusier built a chapel of pure sculpture: anti-functional, anti-structural. Then circular plans returned, and other tight geometrical shapes, and tents, sails and cylinders. The New Brutalists set out to return to base—to rid architecture of anything pretty or pretentious, and the New Ornamentalists ridiculed them and made a determined effort to retore ornament to its traditional position. Thus various frilly details returned, and then rounded arches in trios, and then arcades of pointed arches. And all these things were in good architects' work. The old arbiter, Good Taste, was reappointed. What was happening in the work of poorer architects where even that arbiter was unknown, is too awful to mention. By this time, about 1960, the old European masters of modern design were decisively dethroned and utter anarchy ruled in the world of architecture.

You might believe that it still rules. But I think it is just possible now to see in the chaos a hint of the form that the evolution of modern architecture is taking, and despite much visual evidence

2

to the contrary I believe that the form is essentially good. I see a discipline returning to modern architecture, and a regrowth of artistic and intellectual convictions after a rather silly season, and thus a return to a worthwhile cause, and more good conflict.

There will be a reader who objects that I make too much of artistic and intellectual convictions, for building is a tough industry which recognizes its artistic and social responsibilities for hardly more than one hour a year during speeches at the annual dinner. I reply that this often brutal and always mercenary industry is, in fact, involuntarily guided at a remote distance by intellectual argument and artistic passion beyond its ken. Every structure and shape that building technology makes has come painfully through a decade or so of architectural soul-searching by the leaders, the creative men of world architecture. Since this is the twentieth century when any new idea is likely to be flashed round the world as fast as thought, so every new thought by the international hierarchy inevitably passes down through many levels of profession and trade to touch in time every humblest builder's most ordinary cottage-villa. Thus one of my other potential critics, who will say that I speak as if the world of architecture is without different regions and folk techniques, is also answered. But if I ignore regional variations I do it with regret. I enjoy them, and deplore most 'international' hotels, except for dinner. But any national styles that appear nowadays, and from now on, inevitably will be linked to the world chain of architectural thinking, to international beliefs about what architecture is, and what it should be doing at any moment. The practice of architecture is undoubtedly loaded with questions which I ignore here, but in fact all of them can be answered—morally if not legally—by answering only one question: what is the aim of it all? Yet this is a question seldom asked and often evaded. It is the one which I, naïvely, have tried to answer.

Remote as they may seem, the metaphysics of design reach out to everyone, at work and play and in the family living-room, often in breathtakingly quick time. Thus the importance of the puzzle of architecture.

Parts of this book have appeared before in the *Architectural Review*, England, and *Harper's Magazine*, U.S.A.

Melbourne, 1965.

New Ornamentalism

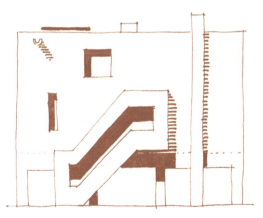

New Brutalism

Part One | PROBLEMS

Architecture is the only art that always starts with a puzzle. Of course other arts have their problems and other artists may pace the floor biting on a nail or a pencil, or with eyes closed and ears shut may try to drag a motif or phrase out of a personal void. But these people have erected their own targets. Their problems are of expression or technique and their anguish is self-inflicted. An architect knows their problems, and may suffer as much as any of them in the course of design. But at the birth of each project, at least, the problem is not set by himself but by his client.

To some extent every client is a patron. Often this is quite conscious and explicit, the client sincerely wanting the architect to produce a fine example of his art. He has first, however, a puzzle to be solved, a practical matter, a useful shelter of some specific kind to be made as efficiently as possible. The puzzle is familiar, yet different with every new project that comes to the architect. The kind of shelter required may be quite new to him, and even if it is in a field with which he is familiar the relevant regulations and the budget and the available materials and the personalities involved may all be different this time, so that previous experience will be of only limited help.

So the client gives the architect a commission and the architect accepts a problem, commonly called just that in his drawing office. Each architectural problem at first is something like a jig-saw puzzle spilled out of its box. The pieces of information lie in an uncommunicative jumble, some face down: the budget, the required accommodation, the likely costs as known from experience, the desirable mood to be created, the legal restrictions, the site limitations, the building regulations, the town-planning considerations, the predilections of the client, and so on.

Now, the object of the puzzle may be stated quite simply. It is merely to combine all the factors into a whole: one artistic form built so spontaneously and convincingly that it might appear to belong to some natural or intellectual pattern of creation. But since modern architecture tore up the traditional guide pictures to the puzzle the architect usually can see at first no single glint of dominant colour nor suggestion of shape on which he could start building his design. As he starts to turn the pieces over and stir them tentatively he has not and cannot safely have any idea of the form of the solution. Yet he knows from experience that, no matter how confusing and unrelated the pieces now seem to be, there is at least one solution which before long he will come to recognize as the correct solution. As soon as he can find this, his own correct guide picture, the pieces will appear to fall into interlocking place as inevitably as the centre of a jigsaw picture once the four edges are fitted together. This guide picture image will stay before him through the hopeful hours of preparation of sketch plans, though the early bold scribbles and the last satisfying details of planning. Soon it will take its first concrete form in perspective drawings or a pristine model, and the puzzle will be solved. Only the problems of building will begin.

Probably no building has ever been designed which did not reach this 'sketch' stage with the architect still confident that his guide picture or vision was the right one. Then follows the task of preparing working drawings, weeks or months on the boards while every detail of structure, equipment and finish is designed or selected, and recorded in reams of drawings and specification notes. This is the final step of design: the productive period when a piece of architecture, something like a symphony but little like any other work of art, is composed and formalized in every important detail, but only in the mind of its designer. The effect remains secret from others. After this period, after the drawings are completed, the rest is only prodigious routine: a matter of building to the plans, a business with problems enough of its own, but administrative and corrective rather than artistic ones. For after the plans are done little or no room is left for improvisation or further artistic development.

Most architects succeed in reaching this stage still holding confidence in the guide vision which they extracted from the puzzle pieces at the beginning. Occasionally doubts crowd in over the drawing board when pieces refuse to fit together, though usually these difficulties can be dispelled by modifications to the central idea. But sometime after this—as the steel rises or when the elaborately contrived finishes are being fitted together, or later, perhaps on the very afternoon of the official opening— sometime the architect will tell himself, or a friend or critic will tell him, that his guide vision was not the only possible one after all, and was not even the best possible one. There were other solutions to the problem which would have been just as practical

8

but perhaps less stylized, or more relaxed, or more imaginative, or more realistic, or less classic, or less romantic, or less pretentious. Was he right in selecting the image he did? Then the architect is confronted again with a puzzle much more complex and disturbing than any design problem: the problem or puzzle of architecture itself.

For architecture is puzzling at many levels. On the lowest and broadest plane, to the non-enthusiasts, the millions who want from it nothing but convenient shelter, it presents the simplest yet in a sense the greatest puzzle of all. Simply this: Why is it? Why all the styles and mannerisms, all the thousands of different attempts presumably to do the same thing, to make a building beautiful? If it is generally agreed that the Greeks achieved architectural beauty on the Acropolis, two thousand four hundred years ago, could not architects have discovered by now whatever secrets or techniques were involved? Why are they still fumbling, and producing so few attractive buildings and so much indefensible ugliness? (Not to mention the cost of it and the troubles they can give you with inefficient air-conditioning.) Why are architecture and architects necessary? Would not the world be better off with a greater number of business consultants to plan circulation patterns, feeding instructions to efficiently organized teams of thoroughly trained technologists, skilled technicians and honest bricklayers? In case any aesthete should feel in some superior way that appearances might be overlooked by such a practical group, let it be said at once that there could be room in the team for a taste consultant. For even on this lowest and broadest plane of architectural appreciation appearances are never entirely overlooked. Here the criterion is the matter known as taste. It is not very well understood and rarely is any attempt made to practise it, but it is accepted as something vaguely nice in the Western background, like religion, which one can legitimately fall back upon in emergencies provided one drops a silver coin in the collection plate every so often.

This rather cynical and uncultivated attitude to design may be familiar and understandable; and yet in the case of the Parthenon at least there does seem to be something more to building than the proposal for a practical team assumes. There is something else which even the most unenchantable observer can sense.

9

The few stone walls and decapitated columns left standing among the bleached rubble of the Acropolis convey to us still the spirit of a civilization in a more personal and impressive way than the message of a painted urn or even of the written word. This is the puzzling thing: there is some magic that can be found in the juxtaposition of some building stones, in their masses and spaces, not entirely explainable by historical and sentimental associations. There is some magic in the boulevards of Paris, not entirely attributable to the nightclubs and the wine. Something of the same magic may be sensed at rare intervals closer to home, even in some new construction; anyone will admit to some beauty in one or two recent buildings. But why should this quality be so rare, and so difficult and costly to buy? Thus the puzzles on the broadest level are all whys.

On the narrower plane of the enthusiasts: people of taste, amateurs and fanciers of architecture, these naive questions are not asked. Here the question is not *why?* but *what?* It is understood that beauty is not a measurable, saleable commodity that can be added in any quantity to taste after efficient businessmen and technicians have designed a building. (Alternatively, if any quality that can be so added is describable as beauty, then beauty is not the essential element of architecture.) On this plane the observer is sympathetic but none the less puzzled: What is architecture seeking? To an interested amateur who wants to understand its aspirations and methods, the art of building can be a bewildering enigma. One can understand that the great gold stone Parthenon, cast against the blue Grecian sky, was a product of its own remote civilization, and now has little or no reference to our building methods and social requirements. But should we not be trying in our own way to achieve the same kind of result, the same kind of artistic response in the viewer?

In the 1950s the man of taste looked up at the first of a long line of grey-green glass office towers and was puzzled. He knew that this uncommunicative block was a genuine product of modern technology. It was sensible. It did not positively offend his taste. Yet he could find no word to describe it more polite than 'interesting'. He much preferred to turn back to the eighteenth century when he could use the word 'glorious'. The realization of this anomaly gave him no pleasure for he did not wish to rely on

nostalgia; he wanted to live happily with the art of his own time. He wanted to like the skyscrapers, but they only disturbed or bored him. He wondered where was the art in such monuments to technology. He could see that they might have pleasant proportions and colour, if done by men of taste, but this was hardly enough. If architecture were no more than this, how could a man like Nikolaus Pevsner, a distinguished authority surely, say that 'architecture is the most comprehensive of all visual arts and has a right to claim superiority over the others'? How can art exist, how can it hope to flourish, under the suffocating necessity to be useful?

The very foundations of architecture are riddled with such elementary questions, for unlike all the other arts architecture cannot be explained simply by saying that it is a medium for communicating experience. As an art it is burdened inescapably by its practical and social responsibilities. These do not appear in any way to damp the desire to communicate of those who choose this medium of expression. The responsibilities may inhibit the freedom to communicate but they also mean that the communication is put under the noses of captive recipients in a way that is quite unique among the arts.

Many of the puzzles lie in the way of reconciling the architect's natural desire to communicate some personal emotional or intellectual experience with his practical and social responsibilities. To students, in whom a desire to communicate and an awareness of social responsibilities are inclined to be high and uncontaminated by concern for practical realities, the search for a personal reconciliation of this conflict, to find a convincing way ahead between egotism and community service, is one of the major puzzles of architecture.

At times in the past none of these puzzles existed. The builders of the cathedrals and the architects of Georgian England, for example, may have experienced the individual philosophical and technical problems of any artist, but neither they nor their patrons had any fundamental doubts about the direction and aim of their work. Architecture presents such difficulties now because for more than a century it has gone without accepted codes of behaviour, without canons of criticism even among the *cognoscente*, without any agreed yardsticks for judging genuine achieve-

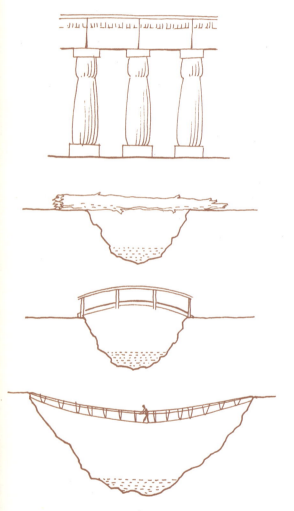

ment. The scale of values of the man in the street, based on the bodily comfort which a building promises, has no common point with the scale of values adopted by most of the world's small circle of recognized architectural critics, in whose company building becomes the most intense, not to say esoteric, of all art forms.

Certainly there are a few rules, a rough basic sort of grammar of acceptable design practice that can be taught and learned. The delicate operation of the fine balance of design propriety, or good taste, so dimly recognized at the popular level, grows to major significance on the narrower plane of the enthusiast, or architecture fancier. To a man who believes with all modesty that he has taste there are no artistic problems. His eye, bolstered by background and conditioned by experience of good things, tells him all he wishes to know. Applied to social intercourse, good taste is a negative term meaning absence of offence. In architecture it means this, but also a little more. Thus the educated architecture fancier reacts instinctively against too many colours or too much shape or too busy a collection of ornamental trifles. But he knows also that slavish copying or reproducing from history or from fashionable leaders of the moment is not to be taken seriously. He expects a touch of originality. He is, however, respectful of style. Good taste in architecture requires some degree of visual or photographic memory. The proud possessor retains in his mind images of the major historical and modern styles, based on memories of shapes and proportions and ornaments and details. He knows by visual experience how much these may be distorted in the interests of variety without destroying the style image.

Taste has other more positive rules, apart from style. The architecture fancier knows that every structure must be self-explanatory and every element must display some conviction and authority. This rule begins with the most elementary of structural problems: how to bridge a gap or space. A flat, straight beam lying across the top of two supports goes unquestioned by the eye, whether it is the short stone lintel of the Egyptians, the long steel beams of today, or a log fallen across a creek. And a humped bridge is even more acceptable to the cautious eye for it is more eloquent of the stresses involved and suggests a margin of safety in its upward curve, whether in a classical arch or a modern shell-concrete vault. Again, in certain circumstances, a sagging suspended shape may be entirely self-explanatory and satisfying, whether in an ancient grass rope bridge over a Tibetan gorge or in the Golden Gate bridge at San Francisco. The flat lintel, the arch, and the catenary, or draped, curve—all are strong, direct formal statements of elementary structure, and all have been the basis of more than one style image. There have been countless variations of the arch, and a few of the drape. But one kind of shape which has never spawned a style is a composite: a bridge or beam or roof combining both raised and draped curves in one snake-shape. Visually striking though it may be, the S-shape is less successful than any of the pure bridge shapes because it looks less trustworthy to the simple and naturally suspicious eye.

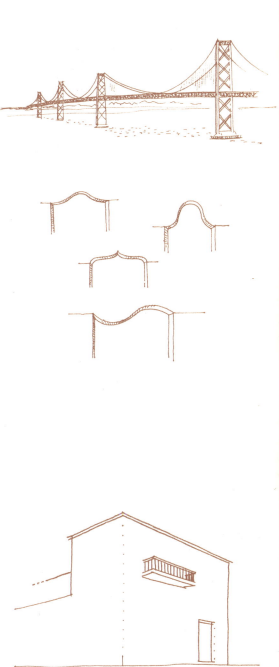

The indecisive snake-shapes do not present a convincing argument for their being. Without question, an S-curve can be built in a thoroughly stable way, yet if the humped curve is correct for its part of the task in hand how can the draped section of the curve also be correct? One must be a less satisfactory solution than the other, and thus the whole is suspect. Why the change of heart that apparently overtook its creator sometime during the course of the design process? The man of taste understands why this shape has no attraction for him. It is indeterminate and weak, and even if there is some secret structural reason for the wave, still the vacillating form has no visual explanation. It is apparently there for effect only; in short, for show. It is therefore a vulgar thing and should be shunned.

The educated fancier of architecture, or man of taste, realizes also that his eye demands some functional justification, however slight, for every appendage. For instance, no one of taste or sensibility could accept in any style an inaccessible balcony, however beautifully designed it was or however artistically placed on the building facade. Yet the eye of taste is easily satisfied. This question of visual justification is not to be confused with the moralities of the Functionalist movement. If there is any sort of hole in the wall behind the balcony most men of taste will be only too happy to accept the deception, no matter how unexpected, unprivate or uncomfortable such a balcony would be

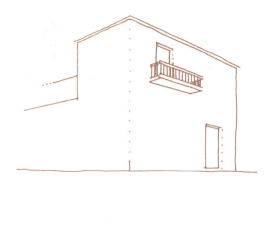

in reality. All that matters to the unprofessional eye is that the balcony looks as if it could be used if necessary. That is the degree of functional justification demanded by good taste.

The educated enthusiast also appreciates the existence of certain natural laws in the behaviour and treatment of building materials: simple rules of right and wrong. He realizes, for instance, that it is wrong to imitate. It is wrong to try to copy the shapes of stonework in timber, or those of concrete in brick, if only because those who do frequently finish with a split or cracked building. It is a wrong use of tiles or slates or shingles to make a roof of them so dashingly low-pitched that it will leak in the first storm. It is an abuse of steel if one makes it so elegantly slender that it collapses under the mayor at the official opening; and therefore conversely it is an equal abuse to make steel unnecessarily obese. Inevitably any designer develops a respect for materials and a visual taste for good construction, and on such pedestrian observations as these a noble pyramid of material morality has, in fact, been built up in architectural theory. This culminates in the concept that all materials have their own integrity, which should be respected almost as scrupulously as if they had stepped from the vegetable and mineral provinces into the animal kingdom.

While the ordinary enthusiast, the intelligent observer of architecture, may not be especially interested in scaling that pyramid, usually he will accept the professional dictum that the difference between right and wrong ways with materials is apparent in some subtle ways even to technically uneducated eyes, resulting in good or bad visual reaction—that is, in beauty or ugliness. He sees a disturbing concoction of tapered columns and oblique beams in the entrance canopy to an urgent commercial bowling alley and he is not surprised to be told by an engineer that the reason it disturbs him is that the taper of the columns runs the opposite way from that dictated by statics, and the obliqueness of the beams is capriciously contrary to a logical solution.

Guided by these and other similar timeless rules in the grammar of design, the educated enthusiast, the man of taste, watched the birth and growth of a twentieth-century architecture. He saw nearly all the things he held to be important in architecture discarded: first the sheet-anchor styles of history, then all ornament, then the rules that went with the styles, of symmetry and balance, composition and proportion. But gradually he accepted all of this and came to recognize other attractions in the rectilinear forms, the glass, and the plain solid slabs of walls and roof. After half the century passed he became accustomed to the plain, direct language, and he dutifully accepted the United Nations Secretariat in New York, a huge but expressionless glass box, as a symbol of international co-operation after World War II. By 1956 or so he even learned to distinguish between the different glass boxes, noting that Gordon Bunchaft's Lever House on Park Avenue was more refined that the United Nations building, that Mies van der Rohe's apartment blocks on Chicago's Lake Shore Drive were finer in technical detail and interrelation, and that Osborn McCutcheon's I.C.I. House in Melbourne had a clever separation of service and office areas—a blind tower of lifts and lavatories almost detached from the side of the all-glass tower—which were nicely complementary to each other in strength and proportion, like male and female. The architecture fancier was thus able to extract a little enjoyment out of the glass boxes by playing at the old game of taste, although it was still difficult to recapture anything like the enthusiasms of the ornamented ages.

Up to this point modern architecture had evolved comparatively gently. Now it was on the verge of a first major shift in foundations to a new philosophical stand. Even when a new monumental phase of modern architecture appeared in strength about 1958 it did not displace the glass box; it developed independently. In the financial hearts of cities and out on the industrial fringes commercial building generally remained satisfied with the box made of curtain walls. Business continued building it in great numbers with varying admixtures of fashionable vulgarity around the entrance foyers. To many casual observers and careless lay critics the glass box still represents the whole of modern architecture even to this day, though in fact it represents only the first half of the century. The spare, square work that was labelled the International Style ceased long before 1960 to interest the architectural creators or serious critics. After the early fifties this style was not fed with any significant quantity of creative ideas. It was merely heaped with sterile, superficial, semi-advertising

Lever House

I.C.I. House

15

notions. Nevertheless it carried on. Even now the biggest share of the foreseeable future of building still clearly belongs to relatives of the curtain wall: to standardized, industrialized, repetitive kinds of building. But this part of the future will be pursued without the architect who had fought on its behalf against tradition and prejudice for half a century. Once the glass box was popularly accepted it needed him no longer. Control of it passed from the architect's hands into those of the backroom boys of technology. There were a few seats in the back room for clever designers and stylists working alongside the technologists, polishing and perfecting the details of the glass cube, trimming its metal frames and devising pleasant surface treatments for the panels that concealed the piped creature comforts. But there was no seat in that room for the architect, let alone a throne. No scope for the architect's kind of exploration and invention was left in the glass box. He is not wanted now in the laboratories where its development continues, and he does not really want to be there.

In the late fifties when this situation was emerging, the future of architecture was in some doubt. For a moment it looked as if architects had simplified their work to the point of having no job left. Here was perhaps the greatest problem that ever faced the art of architecture: was it expendable? Was there a place, in the new world of air-conditioned shelter technology, for the traditional kind of architect, for his poetry, invention and acrobatics? Or was the modern world inexorably taking building along the track of the horseless carriage into the mass-production market where the lowest common denominator of taste ruled?

Without much doubt it can be said that the answers ultimately will be affirmative. Probably there will be no place for the artist architect in the last chapter of building. Architecture one day will be an interest for archaeologists only, an art whose medium became obsolete like the radio play and the silent film. Yet that may not be for a century or more, and in the meantime there is useful work for an architect to do. Nevertheless, the success of the qualities propagated by the pioneer architects of the twentieth century—the impersonal, universal qualities of precise machines —began to assume a somewhat menacing shape to creative architects of the mid-century. Like Frankenstein or Dr Jekyll the architects watched helpless as the glass box took on a life of its own. And as they watched they began to realize that the cult they had fostered, of impersonal, machine-like universality, no longer held any magic for them. Gradually the contrary values grew more dear to them. While it was still necessary and economically possible to build one building at a time, until the future day when mass-production would eclipse the art of individual building, some special solution to each particular problem of shelter seemed called for. Indeed some valid statement of appropriate character, fresh and unique for each new building, might be considered the only justification for the continuance of a partly-obsolete profession.

From this mood grew the second phase of modern architecture and a sudden spectacular increase in the number of personal expressions and imaginative shapes and personality cults around new star architects. One time about the mid-fifties the men of taste were fairly confidently settled in acceptance of the style that had grown in the first half of the century. They looked forward to an unexciting but pleasant consolidation of the style during the next generation or so. They were just a little concerned at the apparent absence of brilliant younger men to ensure a proper consolidation, at the fact that no solid second line of generals seemed to be lining up ready to take charge upon the retirement of the old leaders—Frank Lloyd Wright, Le Corbusier, Mies van der Rohe and Walter Gropius. Then within a few weeks, or so it seemed, hardly longer than the time between issues of the style-sensitive journals, the outlook abruptly changed and there were generals everywhere. Not just four four-star generals, as in the second quarter of the century, each with a world following for his own personal manner within the style, but suddenly hundreds of one-star generals, some popping up in places previously unheard of for architecture, everyone his own *avant-garde*, and everyone apparently galloping in a different direction. In a few years around 1960, years of what might be called violent evolution, the plainness and directness left modern Western architecture. Plastic forms appeared, but more plastic than ever before. Ornamentation returned in various new guises. Some buildings retired behind grilles reminiscent of Eastern fairy tales. In place of the acquired delight in great white planes of concrete or green

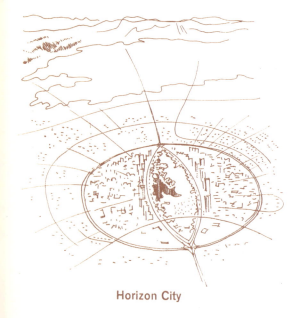

Horizon City

mirrors of glass, some architects suddenly showed a regard for every smallest piece of structure, brought framework out of hiding and proudly displayed all elements, wherever possible separately, spaced apart as far as possible. Yet, sometimes literally on the other side of the fence, the enthusiast could follow also a movement diametrically opposed to the piecemeal approach. He saw large buildings ruthlessly subjected to a single discipline of a strictness such as was never before applied architecturally even in the days of the Inquisition: single thoughts stretched to contain whole cities, as in the case of Lucio Costa's plan for Horizon City in Texas. In place of straight lines and simple planes one found intricate criss-crossing beams and posts, or sails of concrete, or laceworks of shadows.

It was clear that the second half of the century was already kicking over the traces of the first half. It seemed now in retrospect that the first half had not been especially exciting, except at the time in its struggle against Edwardian taste. It left few monuments. But, to be fair, it had not tried to build monuments. It was too busy fighting. The first half of the century was comparatively monotonous artistically because its strength was used in clearing a way of freedom for a creative architecture. In this it had succeeded. Now, with the glass box behind it, the art of architecture again had roughly as many styles and as many creative people as the arts of painting or music, with roughly as large a range of expression, including buildings as far from conventional as electronic music, dribble painting or junk sculpture. Each year during the late 1950s the official award lists of the architectural institutes carried an increasing diversity of unfamiliar forms. More and more of the disciplines for which the pioneers had fought were cast aside. Fewer and fewer rules seemed to be left intact for the man of taste to cling to. He may have had quite a wide understanding of what should *not* be done in the making of architecture. He still may have been able to derive some harmlessly malicious enjoyment from the exercise of this knowledge in observing the blunders or the deliberate perversity of designers with less than his own degree of taste. But still none of these negative warnings helped greatly towards a positive understanding of the central puzzle.

Among the new leaderless rabble of styles, which could be

18

accepted as valid? How or why did many of the outlandish effects differ in essence from some vulgar commercial building which was weirdly shaped simply to attract one's attention?

What—asked the few architecture fanciers who still looked at buildings on Sundays—What is architecture?

Oddly enough, in view of the apparent confusion in the ranks of architecture, the professional man as a rule has no great difficulty in putting an answer to the layman's key question. Every reasonably sensitive and experienced architect knows what architecture is. He knows that the timeless principle of good design may be stated quite simply. It is integrity: wholeness, unity. It is in the creation of a microcosm of Nature, of truth, by the arrangement of the functional and material components of a building.

On the professional plane the question is not *what?* but *how?* The architect wants to build with the conviction of the Greeks and the Goths but to be honest to his modern business-like world at the same time.

He need not subscribe to the austere cult of Functionalism to know that his building must first shelter effectively; that is, it must be shaped overall and planned in detail to function, not just to appear to be capable of functioning. Similarly it must withstand the elements. He reads some of the minor hints and tips of Nature in her simplest lessons that he can understand and apply, as in the gothic structure of a tree. He realizes dimly that all the secrets he needs to know are somewhere before his eyes in organic growth patterns. He regards animal beauty as some sort of unattainable goal and guide, and he notes an almost comparable perfection of form in the works of designers of some machines, notably vehicles which ride on or in fluids. In his own work he finds that the more he is led away by some geometrical or emotional fancy from direct planning solutions and unambiguous structural methods, the more difficulties he has during construction. He finds, often by sad experience, that it is wrong to force planning systems and structural methods against their grain. Somehow he must mould them in sympathy with their grain so that they will follow whatever theme evolves in his mind. Thus the core of the architectural puzzle presents itself to him most directly in this form:

Puzzle—Use the sternly practical business of providing bodily shelter as a medium for artistic expression.

The artistic exercise is no lighter in a holiday house than in an opera house. The ancient game of architecture demands from modern architects visual communications no less intense or revealing than any carried by the most uninhibited media of art. Yet if anything other than useful elements are introduced the player is disqualified and must return to sculpture.

This is the basis of the fascination with the puzzle. One must accept it like a maddeningly irresistible wooden parlour puzzle with faith that a solution is possible. Though no one has ever actually, completely, succeeded before, neither has anyone ever been able to prove that it cannot be solved, But how to do it? Every professional architect has his own method of attacking the basic inconsistency. The great majority are led by bread-and-butter reasons to such stern concentration on the practical business that they have no time or talent left for communication of any visual ideas. However it must not be thought that in doing this they have necessarily forgotten, renounced or misread the conditions of the game. Sometimes they attempt to add the other side of architecture towards the end of the process, in the form of non-functioning elements, and thus they are disqualified. Sometimes they make no pretence of wishing to create anything but a commercially satisfactory shelter using appropriate empirical structural methods with a sensible application of the latest manufactured components: standard windows, doors, facing panels, and so on, all selected with moderate imagination and care in regard to their neatness of appearance as well as their practicability. The better educated architects of this school fortunately have sufficient taste as a rule to stop designing at this point, having enough experience to know the dangers of decorative additions. Thus most buildings outside the crassly vulgar jungle, most buildings which take themselves seriously, are practical but are not articulate.

Yet by no means all. At the opposite end of the scale from the dull glass boxes there is another small, scattered and diverse category of buildings, equally unbalanced, but with the load on the other side.

A well-known example of this group is a house built between

1951 and 1957 for the garden-loving Bavinger family of Norman, Oklahoma, by the architect Bruce Goff. This house he conceived as a section of luxuriously planted garden, with pool and paved areas, over which he erected a sort of permanent tent made of a rough stone wall spiralling in and upwards round a central steel mast under a semi-glazed roof. In the big fluid space so enclosed the architect hung shallow saucers, each about ten feet in diameter, wrapped entirely in soft carpet and reached by means of a stair that spiralled around the central core. These saucers hanging in a garden space were 'rooms'—bedrooms playroom, lounge, studio. Part of an upper bedroom saucer and most of the top studio saucer broke through the stone wall, since at their elevation the tent had contracted to a diameter too narrow to contain them. Thus they enjoyed some fresh air as well as sharing the internal garden space. In this building Bruce Goff abstracted from the comparatively complex requirements of family and plant life a single form-thought, artistically whole and complete, poetically complicated and even mysterious in its visual quality, with its odd mixture of materials from rubble rocks to guy wires, and yet intellectually satisfying almost to the extent of seeming inevitable under the circumstances. This house was as moving, revealing and communicative of the ideas and emotional approach of its architect and its owners as it was impractical in its lack of privacy, uncomfortable in its cavalier attitude to gravity, and reactionary to the progress of building technology in its perverse selection of rustic materials.

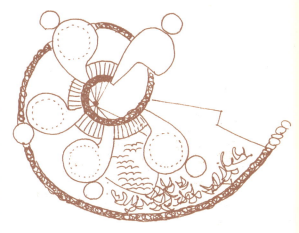

The Bavinger house: plan and section

The Bavinger house may be singularly far out from the central line of everyday building, but it represents a body of architectural thought devoted to the communication of ideas and the expression of feelings, at the expense, if need be, of practicality. Le Corbusier encouraged this movement greatly with his chapel at Ronchamp which came at the post-war time of hesitation and self-examination.

The works of this school have in common the fact that they are conspicuously once-only pieces, each one designed for a specific purpose and usually for specific people. While the techniques of mass-production aid the larger body of inarticulate materialist building, other branches of modern technology are continuously increasing the freedom and scope of architects at this Expres-

Sydney Opera House

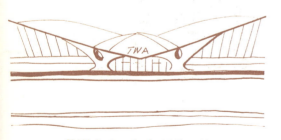

T.W.A. terminal at Idlewild

sionist end of the scale. The development of shell concrete in the 1950s seemed to offer the architect a new medium as plastic and responsive as anything to be found in a sculptor's studio; any shape devised by the architect and demonstrable in plasticine could be enlarged to monumental size by the use of shell concrete, or so it seemed. When faith in the free possibilities of shells was at its height in 1956 Joern Utzon, a brilliant young Dane, entered a design in the international competition called for Sydney Opera House. He showed the two auditoria and their awkward tall stage lofts covered by high shells or sails of concrete, billowing as if caught by the salty winds of the harbour, looking as light as canvas. Eero Saarinen was one of the competition judges. He pounced on Utzon's free, dashing pencil sketches and without hesitation put their flimsy sheets on the top of the pile of meticulously drafted conventional-modern entries on their stiff cardboard mounts. Utzon's design, with its skilful simplification of the planning problems and its glorious sails flying above was a thing after Saarinen's own heart. It exemplified the most advanced mood of the 1950s. When the design came to be constructed years later, however, shell concrete was found to be unsuitable. The sails were disciplined from free shapes into spherical segments and made in pre-cast sections. By then Eero Saarinen was dead.

In the meantime numerous others had exciting successes with only slightly more disciplined and geometrical shapes in the years approaching 1960, most notably in the twisted concrete churches of the Mexican, Felix Candela. At the same time exploitation of the principle of tension—support by suspension from above rather than by the compression of props from below—began to add new possibilities in form to every imaginative architect's repertoire. A notable building of this period, the T.W.A. terminal building at Idlewild Airport, New York, by the late Eero Saarinen, was significant because for the first time the complicated functions of a busy commercial public building were subjected to a free, imaginative, expressive form. Its spreading wings expressed the idea of flight and it was popularly called the 'Giant Bird'. Skilful interior planning by its experienced architect succeeded in making the giant bird function satisfactorily, yet clever as it was Saarinen's *tour de force* failed to strike the profession of

22

architecture as a timeless solution to the puzzle. It had too many odd shapes and redundant spaces that failed to convince functionally and were in fact clearly made for sculptural effect only, with little reference to the well-being of those it sheltered. It seemed indeed to be almost in the Bavinger house category, as far away from a centrally balanced solution as any of the numb glass boxes.

The profession still had faith that a balanced solution could be found, still entirely functional and undecorated, yet communicative of ideas, something balanced sensibly between a giant bird and a glass cage. Thus, encouraged by men like Saarinen and goaded a little by men like Goff, architects at this time began to break away from the once-solid ranks of the modern movement, and the multitude of new forms which so greatly confused the lay observers began to appear. Traditional shapes were revived, though often in disguise. Decoration reappeared and was welcomed by some who were considered to be *avant-garde*. The writings of Adolf Loos were dug up and re-examined. Early in the movement, in 1908, Loos had written a famous essay, 'Crime and Ornament', which was one of the unread gospels of the modern movement before 1950. Now it *was* read, but critically, and turned inside out, and ridiculed. Philip Johnson, the brilliant New York architect of many tastes, in 1961 made a notable statement reflecting the general renunciation of rationalism. In a letter to Dr Jurgen Joedicke, a critic of the American counter-revolution, he wrote: 'The entire modern movement—looked at as an intellectual movement dating from Ruskin and Viollet-le-Duc, going through the Werkbund, Bauhaus, Le Corbusier to World War II—may be winding up its days ... structural honesty seems to me one of the bugaboos that we should free ourselves from very quickly ... I am old enough to have enjoyed the International Style immensely and worked in it with the greatest pleasure ... But now our age is changing so fast. Old values are swept away by new with dizzying but thrilling speed. Long live Change!'

Thus the pieces of a general modern guide vision which had been laboriously built up over half a century were wildly scattered again. The puzzle was thrown open to every individual architect, and he was left alone to find his own images in a field of possibilities made wider, more challenging and more puzzling than ever before by the new structural processes.

As if this were not hard enough! Yet always the puzzle of designing a single building is only the start of an architect's design problems. It is merely the puzzle of shaping a single flower. But this flower will bloom among the weeds of modern industrial-commercial development. The architect can never ignore the rest of the sour garden. His building is linked to the traditions and mores of its region and its nation. It will inevitably affect the area in which it is built, physically by increasing the traffic problem and the shadows, visually by the degree it contrasts, blends or clashes with the surroundings. The architect is held responsible by the community for the effect of his building on the neighbourhood. Sometimes he himself sees his responsibilities extending far beyond this, and he takes on his back a part of the burden of the wholesale ugliness of the modern world. He feels an indirect responsibility even for the thoughtless mass of those many buildings which are made without any professional guidance, and beyond those for the blight of signs, billboards and service stations.

If an architect, with great pains, can sometimes succeed in making a building of integrity, its surroundings frequently are so hideous as to make his little effort appear naïve and almost ridiculous. The twentieth century, which started with such visual promise, has turned out to be the ugliest in history. Modern industrial-commercial man has grown up to be more calamitously inartistic than the man of any previous era. He combines a flashy taste for artificiality with the most efficient means of satisfying it. He does not recognize the shoddiness of the street of strident colours, with the catchpenny styling and the signs, hoardings, lights, pylons and poles all wrapped up clumsily in great loose tangles of overhead wires. He shapes his towns not for simple usefulness and certainly not with love of them, but always to advertise or symbolize something: a somewhat distorted Georgian Colonial porch symbolizes old-fashioned comfort and a family tree; an exaggerated roof shell advertises a restaurant and its designer's cleverness. Modern man may not like his surroundings, but he is content to accept them. He does not feel obliged to look at them, and the more his attention is solicited the more he condi-

24

tions himself to ignore the visual irritants. He is satisfied by one or two fine avenues and skyscrapers near the centre of town, and by a few crude shallows of architectural expression, such as the provocative gloom of a cocktail lounge, or the sterile dazzle of a supermarket, or the cosiness of woody plastic surfacing in a living-room. Vaguely pleased by a few such appropriate changes in the visual background of his life, he is prepared to overlook the strident mess of the rest of it.

The architect has always felt superior to the popular mess, even while the people unreasonably blame him for it. Unreasonably, because even in enlightened communities most of the visible man-made world is as far removed as the natural world from the control of architects. Yet, as the nominal spiritual leader of building, the architect is still the figurehead from which the public expects a little guidance; and any guidance that has come since the middle of the century has been confused and contradictory.

For nearly half the twentieth century the architects of the International Style did give clear leadership, though at first few enough laymen recognized it as such. But gradually the glass box won reluctant, partial acceptance of some men of taste, as we have seen. It was taken to be at least a symbol of rational building and it appeared set to win over the world eventually. As the movement gathered strength the architects who were marching in the lead looked uneasily over their shoulders and suddenly wondered what they were doing in such vulgar company. They left. Some old generals remained but all their staff officers deserted. Not only the International Style, but the whole movement towards a functional realistic architecture was left without progressive or vigorous leadership. In the latter half of the 1950 decade the brighter young architects wandered far away, and in many different directions. Then the flood of new styles came pouring back, one after another, from numerous small *avant-garde* cults. Visual excitement returned to architecture, and in indigestible quantities. Eventually all ranks of the once optimistic and co-operative march to the future broke up and dispersed. Some architects deliberately and almost proudly raced away from public understanding and sympathy. They had little enough sympathy for each other. They practised and encouraged individuality if not outright

25

indiscipline, and although they felt superior and detached from the popular mess, their own inconsistency set the worst possible example and added to the degeneration of all the man-made environment.

Yet architects collectively and officially were dismayed by the general ugliness that marked nearly every modern community. J. Roy Carroll, a president of the American Institute of Architects, spoke for the conscience of not merely American but of world architects when he said in 1963: 'We would blame the doctors if our people were covered with running sores. If crookedness ruled the courts we would blame the lawyers. So the fifteen thousand architects in America must take the responsibility for ugliness in their communities.'

The architect's ideal site for building is, of course, a natural wilderness in which he can create the one visible monument to mankind. In practice nowadays he rarely has the opportunity to build anywhere that is not surrounded by other buildings, and often as well by advertisements and wires and other urban litter. This is the background against which serious architects usually must plan their creations. Some blind themselves to it and, blocking their ears to the traffic roar, delude themselves that they are still out in virgin country, as Wright did when he planned the Guggenheim Museum in 5th Avenue. In their belief the ordinary urban scene has deteriorated so far that a self-respecting architect must choose between ignoring it and refusing to build at all. The few who hope to pour a little architectural oil of repose on the troubled scene and exercise reserve and understatement are likely to be considered dull and incapable of imagination. A smartly fashionable surface effect will always steal the street scene. Few eyes have time to spend on a restrained work by some conscientious architect dedicated to ridding his design of fashionable insincerities.

As if all this were not disturbing, disillusioning and deflating enough for the poor earnest architect! Yet worse problems beset him.

At this time when all the problems of reconciling the industry and the art, the social responsibilities, the economics and the expression of building, are occupying the attention of architects more urgently than ever before, other difficulties also are reach-

The Guggenheim Museum

ing a climax. There are unpleasant professional complications. During three generations the gentlemanly calling of architecture had been changing in character. The frock-coated clubman who worked almost single-handed and gave imperious directions on the building site was great-grandfather of the modern manager of a considerable business organization involving any number of assistant architects, consulting structural engineers, mechanical, electrical and accoustic engineers and other specialists, as well as draftsmen, accountants and management consultants. The modern architect's work is not greatly different from that of any business administrator, but is complicated by the fact that he still sees himself to some extent as the old autocrat, the lone artist. It has been difficult to adjust. The rate of change was always accelerating, and since World War II it has galloped. Part of the change is technological. Great-grandfather had to concern himself with the properties of hardly more than a dozen humble materials and the trades that accompanied them: masonry, timber, tiles, cast-iron and so on. Today's architect should have a working knowledge of hundreds of materials and dozens of techniques and must try to keep up with the continuous stream of new products and structural methods, or adaptations of old ones, which the engineers and chemists feed to hopeful manufacturers. It is no longer possible for one man to keep the whole glutted bill of fare before his mind's eye as he plans what materials to use. It is no longer possible for one man to have anything more than an intelligent layman's understanding of most of the many specialist technologies involved in a big mechanized building. Yet one man only must be in final control if the building is to work physically, not to say artistically. So the architect tries still to understand all and finally to shape all, just as great-grandfather did.

The technical advances are really of small consequence in comparison with the social changes which have accompanied them in the building industry. Since the new techniques demand not only an architect's understanding but also the comprehension of the man who is organizing their construction, a new race of builder has grown up. In the course of supervising work on the site, the old-time architect expressed his attitude to tradesmen and tradesmanship by breaking off any pieces of carving which appeared less than perfect, or by pushing over, before it set, any masonry which displeased him, while the builder followed behind him cap in hand, and apologized. But his great-grandson faces across the desk a builder who is likely to be wearing a more expensive suit than his own and controlling an organization which employs a greater number of university graduates than there are in the architect's own office.

Then on the rare occasions when great-grandfather came up against a recalcitrant builder and landed in difficulties with extra charges in the final accounts, his client was inclined to take the indulgent view that his architect was after all an artist. That, when all was said and done, was why he had employed him, not to be a businessman. But the modern architect is conditioned to expect that any client who feels in any way injured will automatically resort to the protection offered by the flexible law on professional negligence; and not, let it be admitted, entirely without reason. For surely there has been an abnormally high rate of detail failure in buildings of modern design, ranging from the smoking of some exciting-looking island fireplaces through the leakings of various originally-shaped roofs to occasionally more serious structural subsidence, or the hasty additions of unplanned supports. Modern houses had comic associations long before Jacques Tati's killing parody of them in his film *Mon Oncle*. The movement which was dedicated to the machine seemed to have more than its share of difficulties with machinery, such as air-conditioning. Many of the most respected of the twentieth-century masters of architecture had their nights of sleeplessness worrying over sagging cantilevers or leaking glass roofs, except that some of these men were of such stuff that they could sleep through any- thing. But difficulties have been maddening enough and frequent enough to turn some once-sympathetic clients, now flooded out or smoked out, against the whole idea of the architectural art and the architectural profession.

For most of the failures there were some good excuses. Much of the time the new architecture was, and still is, feeling its way with new techniques and new materials. It would be unreasonable to expect resounding success every time. And it would be wrong to suggest that the twentieth-century movement was especially plagued by these teething troubles. The giant classical domes, the lofty Gothic vaults, the daring Victorian cast-iron, all had their moments of catastrophe. The world would not thank the architectural profession if it stopped looking ahead, and discouraged the taking of first steps into unknown territory. Then another excuse: a great number of the early essays in the new architecture had to be done on the tightest budgets simply because clients with enough spirit of revolution or adventure to commission them were rarely pillars of the establishment with money to burn. In fact many of the brave clients were attracted to the plainness of the modern movement because they expected it to be less costly than traditionally ornamented and complicated forms. The new architects also felt, as a matter of principle, that their work should be cheaper than conventional work. This was implied in the Functionalist-rationalist concept.

On the other hand, it must be admitted that the architect's attitude to technological progress in twentieth-century building has been more compulsive than prudent. The theory of Functionalism had nothing whatever to do with everyday practicalities, and theory usually rules in a revolution. Thus, for instance, the problem of the flat roof always dogged the movement. The International Style had no time for pitched roofs, which represented to revolutionaries a defeatist attitude to the weather. The modern movement stood for the idea that the twentieth century should be able, and surely must be able, to make a material that withstood rain and snow without its having to be pitched at the steep angle which betrayed the inadequacy of tiles, slates, shingles or thatch. So the early twentieth-century architects built flat roofs of the inadequate materials which their infant technology gave them, and before long a great number of them leaked. Soon after the photographs had been taken they spilt brown streaks down the crazed plaster of brick walls that were meant to look, and very briefly had looked, as if made of a superlatively smooth concrete or some sort of plasticized metal. When these failures occurred in a rather monotonous and inevitable way the architects blamed the technologists for their failure to answer what appeared to the architects to be the inescapable challenge of the century: to make a cheap flat roof that worked. Ironically enough, by the time the technologists came up with the right answer the architects had grown tired of the machine-like appearance that demanded the flat roof. They were now quite delighted to be given a rational reason for sloping, curving or twisting the roof. Sometimes they even appreciated an excuse to use shingles.

Architecture may be a mixture of art and science, as the dictionary says, an emotional and intellectual exercise full of questions enough to keep some of its practitioners in discussion and argument long after the painters and playwrights have gone to bed. But to their public, the man or woman who commissions the architect, buys the building and lives inside it, architecture is primarily a practical matter of controlling a craft for comfort, or rather an unruly collection of crafts. A roof flattened prematurely for artistic or purist reasons which leaks water into the master bedroom is not well received. A chimney which makes a strong sculptural feature in a spacious room but smokes heavily during the house-warming party is not appreciated. Nor is a tap on a bathroom wall arranged neatly, symmetrically with the shower rose, so that hot water scalds the arm that reaches in to adjust it. The successful practice of architecture requires training or experience in a thousand similar practical matters. A practical man who is also an artist is required. Every architect is this, so he believes to himself: a poet and practical man, administrator and artist rolled into one. Yet in fact no man can be both; only a little of each. Every famous architect from Michelangelo to Mies and Le Corbusier and Wright have made well-publicized practical mistakes and suffered professional criticism and some degree of popular ridicule as a result. It seems that few buildings can be both perfect in a practical sense and a sheer poetic delight. The former quality demands some degree of familiarity and the latter some degree of novelty. It is no more reasonable to expect a perfect blend of these incompatible qualities than to ask one's morning paper to present the news in evocative blank verse. Nevertheless one may be permitted to hope for the perfect blending, for it is not physically impossible; it could just happen in Utopia. Some buildings of undoubted high poetry, such as Le Corbusier's Ronchamp chapel, can succeed also in being practical only because the practical demands on them are very slight. Every strong statement of architecture has something in it to irritate some practical man who has to use it. But then, in any field of technology new projects have their teething troubles;

30

consider the difficulties of the Comet and Electra planes, and the early rocket failures at Cape Kennedy.

To every man and woman, whether they accept it or not, architecture is more than merely the promise of protective shelter, more than a cosy home or a pleasant place for work and play. It is the only art which they cannot avoid experiencing, an art which may seem to some to be in the doldrums at present, but which finally must be recognized as the ultimate record of civilization. The greatest disservice that an architect can do to his art is to make a practical blunder. Any obscure, difficult or abstract work of painting, music, or prose, has a limited capacity for raising tempers. There may be nothing infuriating in the work itself. Its most incensed critic might be appeased if he saw it in a garret, alone in squalor with its miserable author. The annoying quality grows from the knowledge that some other people derive some enjoyment from the apparently worthless object. If this can be explained by the assertion that those who enjoy it must be idiots, the maddening fact remains that the author, the fraud, receives acclaim from these people, and money. All architecture that is in the least revolutionary raises much of this kind of jealous ire, for without doubt a successful architect is in an enviable position. In *The Status Seekers* in 1959 Vance Packard quoted an attempt to rank occupations in order of prestige. It was conducted by sociologists from the University of Chicago on the basis of a large sample census of households in Chicago. The first occupation in the highest-status group of all was 'Licensed Architects'. Among their peers in this top drawer were federal judges, flag-rank military officers and top-level executives of large national concerns. The profession does not enjoy quite this status in Britain or Australia, but still it has a comfortable degree of prestige, and is also known to be not unrewarding in financial terms for the leaders. Moreover it has a glamour above worldly success. Walter Murdoch once was asked to comment on the state of culture in a suburban munici-pality which advertised for assistant architects and garbage collectors at the same salary. He professed to find no real anomaly in the situation for, after all, a garbage collector should be paid highly for doing such unpleasant work, while surely no one else achieves in this world quite such satisfaction in the act of creation as an architect contemplating his finished building. In sheer bulk the architect's personal creation outweighs all other works of art.

With potential rewards so big, no wonder an architect's creation is examined critically. No wonder practical imperfections raise the impatience and tempers of others who would enjoy an opportunity to carve their name so large on the world. If the architect cannot be bothered, or is unable to get the practical matters right, if he cannot make the reliable shelter which is the first purpose of the exercise, then he has not earned a right to work in this great and enviable medium. He should concentrate on other abstract arts; perhaps painting or music.

If he did, he would be safer. Those other arts are protected by their obscurity and proud disinclination to divulge their intentions. There can be a similar protective indefinition about architecture's artistic aim, and this indeed is what protects some architectural reputations. About one part of a building's aim, however, there can be nothing vague. Whatever else it aims for, a building is required firstly to shelter, to withstand the elements, to provide comfort. When it fails to do so, as indicated perhaps by the rhythmic pings of water dropping into a basin from the living-room ceiling, a building has, without question, failed. Anyone who was not artistically attuned to the design of the building in the first place will see, and will welcome seeing, the unanswerable evidence of failure, and will be doubly maddened, suffering vicariously the righteous indignation of the wronged and wetted client. But anyone who is drawn artistically to the building will tend always to separate in argument the physical failure from the artistic expression: the building construction from the architecture. He will blame the builder, or assistants in the architect's office. If this is not feasible, if it is an inescapable fact that the architect himself made an error of judgment or overlooked a practical necessity, then the friendly critic will have no difficulty in separating philosophically the two duties of the architect. In extreme cases he might be forced to admit that an architect whose concepts he admires could be called, perhaps, accident-prone, but he will still see this man's artistic contribution as something quite apart from the practical imperfections.

So here is another puzzle of architecture: which of these critics is right? Can the art, the ideas, the expression of architecture be separated for purposes of evaluation from the practical side of building? Fortunately this puzzle is answered more easily than most. There are two answers, because there are two kinds of practical imperfection. One kind is separable and the other is indivisible from the artistic act.

For instance, two buildings in the same neighbourhood and built about the same time were insufferably hot in summer, harrowing the owners and infuriating the practical critics who shared the owners' suffocation though they would never have reason to enter either door. Both buildings received awards after being judged by other architects, who examined photographs, as the best of their respective kinds for their year. Scientific investigation disclosed different reasons for the aggravating heat. The first building was a massive masonry block with vigorous sunshading louvres striping the front. The second had an elegant shell concrete vault, so light it appeared almost to fly, with a glass curtain filling the tall void between the vault and the paved entrance plaza below. The first building admitted only a soft glow of reflected sunlight, the second a stream of direct sun, delightful in winter. Now, it appeared that the excessive summer heat in the first building had two main causes. A new patented insulating foam had been sprayed into the roof space. This material was claimed by its manufacturers and confirmed by independent scientists to have qualities exceeding those of the old staple insulating blankets like rock-wool. However, a year after opening, a chemical reaction between the foam and an interesting kind of anti-condensation plastic coating used on the roof material immediately above caused decomposition of the foam. As a consequence the roof was robbed of its insulation and the sun's heat beat invisibly but practically unimpeded through the ceiling. Moreover it appeared that the consulting engineer had miscalculated the heat load on the building, apart from the ineffective roof. He was not to blame, for it appeared that the architect's office had failed to mention to him at any time the kind of machinery which the owners intended installing in the basement. This included two small electric kilns which gushed furnace heat whenever opened, which was often. Consequently all the cooling ducts through the building were little

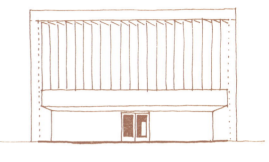

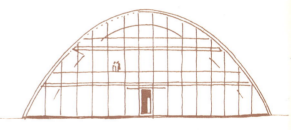

more than half as big as they should have been and the air-conditioning plant, working overtime, sent only ineffectual puffs into the oppressive air.

The second building was not air-conditioned since the owners had instructed from the beginning that their budget would not run to it. Accommodation and appearance were more important to them. In this case there was no difficulty in divining the source of heat. It was, of course, the great window-wall under the elegant concrete shell vault. Inside was a hothouse, suitable during half the year for nothing but the tropical plants by the stairway.

Now as to responsibilities: in the first building the faults were not connected with the architectural concept. The architect was reprehensible for failing to anticipate the chemical interaction of the two materials in the roof space, and for failing to note the significance of the kilns in the basement. But these practical errors, resulting in a maddeningly impractical building, did not reflect against his thought processes during the conception, and did not invalidate his guide vision.

The fault in the second building, on the other hand, was indivisible from the concept. It was there from the first moment in which the guide vision came to the architect. The excessive heat intake through the glass was either something he did not foresee, though this seems unlikely, or a calculated disadvantage. The heat was more than compensated in his opinion by the visual delights which the glass admitted to the building: lightness, airiness, the view, the extroversion of the space, the contrast with the voluptuous curves of the shell concrete.

In both buildings the faults could be corrected, for any building difficulty responds to sufficient money. Not a great deal was required in the second case. An elaborate system of blinds was added in front of the window-wall, reducing the temperature to an acceptable level. The first building presented a more difficult problem, and its solution was more costly. Finally the roof was raised and reliable old-fashioned insulation was inserted: then the air-conditioning was supplemented. Each remedial operation was accompanied by the acrimony and emotional stress that attends these occasions by reason of the lack of clear-cut moral culpability.

In the end the costs of the remedial work were recovered in

different ways. The faults in the first building were declared to be technological errors and the owner had a claim of negligence against his architect. The remedial work was then completed without visible design changes. The architectural integrity of the building was never questioned or threatened. Yet the owner never forgave his architect for the troubles he had caused him, even after the latter had paid for the new insulation. His errors were technical and practical. They threw no discredit on the functional validity of his concept and they were not visible to the occasional pedestrian who stopped across the road to admire the building. They were thus forgivable errors in the artistic sense, but in the professional sense, the sense of the whole architect, they were unforgivable and devastating.

In the second case the faults were integral with the concept, and the owner had no claim against his architect for he had shared with him some of the pleasures of creation and expectation, and had been aware of the area of unprotected glass from the beginning. While the architect escaped a financial claim, the corrective work destroyed his concept. The external blinds substituted a blank solid for the light transparent film conceived in his vision. No pedestrians stopped now to admire this building. Yet the architect and the owner sometimes lunch together still, for whatever shortcomings the former may have as a functional designer he is a practical man. And he knows that the world does not want functional architecture. It wants practical buildings.

While the most remote and romantic designer is often brutally forced to recognize that architecture must first be a practical craft that will house people comfortably, on the other hand the most unvisionary practical man also must admit that what he is pleased to call 'aesthetic considerations' are sometimes justified in overriding the baser practical demands. A perfect blend of the mutually exclusive qualities of poetry and practicality, one that will suit everybody, is a Utopian concept. The first step towards a solution of the puzzle of architecture is a realization that in this imperfect world perfect architecture is impossible. But a good balance that will suit men of intelligence and sensitivity is possible, and that is the best for which one can hope.

The practical errors and failures that are inclined to raise the ire of the public against the architect return to him, of course, and make his life in the workaday office no happier than that of any struggling businessman. Thus most architects, and interested laymen, are inclined to the view that the art of architecture would be a delightfully easy and enjoyable activity if it were not frequently spoiled in practice only by the great difficulties associated with the technical and administrative sides. Laymen frequently regret that architects are not a little less artistic and somewhat more practical, better administrators, better businessmen, while artistic architects sometimes daydream of the delightful life that would be theirs, and of the superb works that they would produce, if only the administrative side of practice were not so taxing.

Yet, notwithstanding the mistakes and the hot tempers, the practical side of building is not the really difficult one. The practice of the art is harder. If not, where are all the artistic buildings? The puzzles of architecture on the professional plane are many and real, and the practical ones are nerve-wracking enough —no practitioner would deny that—yet the real puzzle is still a question of art. How does one make as much poetry as possible out of the practical matters of building: the politics, economics, regulations, structures, finishes, the pipes, wires and water problems? And what kind of man makes a practical poet? Who are architects?

The architect is one in about 25,000, statistically, but this figure takes in great areas of the globe which have big populations and no acquaintance whatsoever with architects. In developed Western countries the proportion is one architect to about three thousand people. The architect is attracted to his profession in the first place by any of a number of different reasons, a love of building being the least common. Most often parents are inclined to divert a child in this direction if they recognize an ability at drawing which falls short of promise as an artist. Other reasons include an ability at making things, or a talent with arranging things in bowls, or with colour. For these reasons a high proportion of girls, sometimes one in every two or three students, start architecture courses. But eventually the architect is male. The girls hold their own in architectural school and often excel. Yet very few become principals in practice and there has been only one woman—Jane B. Drew, who married Maxwell Fry—whose name ever became known internationally independently of her husband's. The reason most boys or girls decide to study architecture is simply its innocuity and ambiguity. It is a nice profession, a clean life: art with soap. Almost anyone with his head screwed on can summon up enough talent in one of its many branches to make a satisfying life of it: perhaps as a specialist in research, or acoustics, or equipment, or as an administrator. It can reward a greater diversity of talent than any other profession can. Therefore it does not really call imperatively to any narrow section of youth. A few gravitate to it for family reasons; a few take up the studies because often, in English-speaking countries at any rate, the architectural faculties in universities are made the easiest to enter. The qualifications are just a trifle lower, a degree seems just a little more accessible. Serious academics of other faculties seldom accept the architects as full brothers. They see them falling somewhere between the engineers and the members of the business administration course.

Whatever their reasons for entering the course, most architecture students soon recognize the spirit of the art, and carry in their knapsacks from second year onwards the 4B pencil of a star architect. Small as may be the opinion held by other academics and by the public for architects as a group, a high degree of glamour, probably exceeding that which attaches to the most distinguished doctor or judge, is associated with the few really creative architects, the two or three of each generation whose design is strong and personal enough to receive public recognition. But of all who enter architecture schools only one in ten thousand achieves such distinction. Only about one in a hundred even manages to reach eminence in his own home town. Only one in about twenty-five becomes a private practitioner with any individual or personally shared reputation. Only one in three eventually works himself up through the ranks of office draftsman to a position of senior executive or partner. In Australia one in seven becomes a public servant: an official architect of some sort in a Commonwealth, State, or local government architectural department where he may achieve an office reputation for detailing joinery or for plumbing diagrams. The remainder leave the profession or become assistants to others who are more fortunate in obtaining commissions. Of those who are so fortunate, or so well equipped for the world in other social ways as to run their own offices behind doors carrying their own names, most are kept busy with a hundred routine jobs other than designing: with tendering and certificates and schedules and accounts, and with extending buildings or remodelling them or demolishing them. Only an hour or two a week, if he is lucky, is spent by the average architectural practitioner in designing even a detail of a building. And the more successful he is in a mercenary sense, the less time he will have to spend on design.

Success may elude most artists in any of the other fields, but this is different. It is the elusiveness of opportunity that becomes the biggest problem of all to the architect. This is the desperate central question of practice: how to get work, a building to design? How to get the chance to express one's taste and the techniques learned at architecture school? (Only the madly optimistic would expect a chance to realize so soon any of those glorious concepts or to put one-tenth-part of the blazing ideals of school-born theory into effect). How to find work in a highly competitive business, already crowded at the top, which still officially observes the old gentlemanly professional ethics and is still led by some genuine gentlemen? The conscientious young architect cannot advertise or tout for work. Without question many of his colleagues do tout, and do engage in all sorts of coarse commercial ruses for attracting clients. But, even if the ethical obstacles were removed, to sink to the level of these colleagues would be no solution for the serious beginner. Clients so attracted are not the men whom a serious architect needs.

There are so many players and the prizes are so few. The great, grinding construction industry, mankind's most impressive activity, is mostly a matter of deadly routine. It demands the services of many people who were trained as architects and who are called, and who call themselves, architects, but whose work has nothing to do with using the architectural medium, the shaping of buildings, for improving people's lives or heightening their experiences. It may be recording social history, continuously, faithfully, solidly, but it can do this without architecture and without architects. After all, much of our social history is pretty dull stuff. A flat, lifeless reflection in the buildings which house it is

38

perfectly appropriate. Building projects that, in the eyes of society, demand professional attention are comparatively few. Most houses and flats, factories and warehouses, small shops and schools and service stations are spilled out of standard moulds by builders or construction companies or prefabrication factories. They open no doors more than a crack to a hopeful architect. Our society does, however, seem to believe that the bigger shops and offices and factories need architectural advice, but only because the mathematics involved might be beyond a builder. Thus when society looks for an architect for such work it is not likely to scan the lists of recent graduates. It wants experience and rocklike reputation.

The number of building projects that demand, according to the popular scale of values, artistic as well as professional attention, is surprisingly small. A parliament house. A city hall. A museum, art gallery or other public building describable as cultural. The bigger office blocks that are conceived for prestige. The churches. The houses of rich or artistic people. These last really keep the young architects of the world from the edge of despair. Yet even in this fascinating but ultimately limiting field it is hard enough to get started. In professional theory the architect should attract clients only by the sheer quality of his executed work, but even when he gets his first opportunity, its result, his first building, is unlikely to be more than promising. Frank Lloyd Wright advised young men to build their first one far out of town.

The architect must have a client, as an actor or a film-director must have a production company, as any worker in an expensive medium needs an employer; and building is the most expensive medium of all. A painter may be disappointed with himself and disgusted with his public but for the price of a sheet of masonite and a few tubes of colour he can still keep working. A writer may continue his experiments on even lower capital outlay, and either of them if dissatisfied with the result can destroy it before another soul sees the awful evidence of immaturity. But what can a serious architect do without clients? Pathetically, he can draw. He can draw ideal buildings, and dream cities: a world remade according to a design idea. And several fine, frustrated architects have made world reputations in that way, including Bruno Taut and Erich Mendelsohn nearly fifty years ago and Paolo Soleri and Frei Otto now. But the world in which these reputations have been made is the little world of architectural theory, and although success here is the most stimulating reward an architect can earn it is also associated with hangover and hunger next morning. The drawing of building designs is a minor medium of expression in itself but is as remotely connected with the art of actual building as, for instance, the art of architectural photography. It is no substitute for the sights, sounds and smells of construction.

Yet despite all this the hundred-thousand architects in the world keep their 4B pencils hopefully sharpened and follow the adventures of the dozen or so in every generation who create an individual style. Every now and then, once a year or so, they do receive a commission of a sort that calls upon them to be real designers, whole architects. Then they look more carefully at the work of the few stars, and they question themselves again about what they really believe.

For the hundred-thousand architects the puzzle of architecture came to a head about the year 1960. The variety produced by the few leaders was by then quite bewildering to any conscientious non-genius who tried to find amongst the world's most publicized work a philosophy to guide his own visions. It came to a head because of the new emphasis on individual solutions at a time when technological developments continued to point urgently in the opposite direction—away from individual solutions to standardization and conformity to the processes of remote factories.

Part Two | REVOLUTION

While the profession of architecture remains in anything like its traditional form each architect will try within the area of free movement left to him to solve each problem in the old way, and this involves a logical progression through a number of comparatively easy steps.

The initial step is to set down a programme. This means studying and analysing the brief supplied by the client. It means also investigating and understanding the background to the problem, and all the requirements, including the unrealized ones, of the people for whom one is building: that is, adding to the puzzle extra pieces, extra problems which the architect believes must be solved in order to produce the best building.

The next step is to scrabble and examine all the puzzle pieces and to draw from them a single unequivocal vision, a form-thought which appears to answer all problems: to conceive a solution in the broadest terms that will guide the design from this point on.

The final step in the design process is the interlocking of the puzzle pieces in accordance with the guide vision: the application of technique—in the drafting room, in the administration office, on the building site—to develop the motivating vision throughout the structure, the finishes and details of a complete building.

Good architecture demands proficiency in all the above steps, as well as in the administrative ones that follow. Without proper attention to the programming the vision will be limited, and without expert technique the vision may never be realized. Nevertheless it is the central step of extracting the vision that shapes the building and gives it whatever expression or feeling or poetry it will have. With experience an architect learns to see in the flash when the image forms an entire building complex in principle, including quite intimate details of structure. At this moment an architect proves his creativity or lack of it. At this moment the medium of architecture finds its tongue and communicates some message in its own unique language of occupiable space, or it remains dumb, an exercise at best in harmonious shapes tastefully filled with interior decoration.

The steps of programming, conceiving and developing are taken one by one in the making of every building, no matter how

The Gothic language

subconsciously, or how inauspicious the occasion. The essential central step is capable of being isolated in the work of the stodgiest professional as easily as in the sketch of a wild-eyed graduate uninhibited by any experience, and in the house of a speculative builder-designer of the dreariest suburban cottage, and in a backyard woodshed nutted out by a do-it-yourself husband. In the course of the design of any once-only structure there is the moment of conception when any shape might happen in the mind of the conceiver. As a general rule the conservative professional consciously makes his conception a moment for reproduction or evocation or well-remembered, well-received, and thus tasteful forms. The spec-builder less deliberately selects by blind habit. The amateur anxiously searches his limited experience for a suitable model to adapt to his limited capacity. In short, all of them seek to recall a suitable established solution to problems of the same general kind as the one in hand. But the active and creative professional designer, good or bad, differs from the others in that he feels intellectually, artistically and morally bound to forget or ignore established images in so far as they will inhibit his freedom to devise the most appropriate solution to the specific problem confronting him.

The right solution for a specific problem can best be found by an unprejudiced eye. Thus one task of the creative architect is to rid his mind of visual precedents while he is searching for a concept. Yet the shape of the puzzle solution that finally springs to mind out of the incoherent jumble of scraps of information given to him by his client, the engineers, and experience, is of course never free from previous associations. It is affected by external influences which change from problem to problem, such as the personality of his client, and the budget. It is, however, most deeply affected by constants which derive from his personal background and his artistic or philosophical approach. These constants tend to hold latent in the back of his mind's eye an overall guide solution to the entire puzzle of architecture. As this general image forms over the years of his work he is said to be developing a personal style.

When most members of a body of architects have similar backgrounds and similar artistic or philosophical approaches producing similar personal styles, then a nameable architectural style is said to be and seen to be in sway in a country or an era.

It records the social story in a coherent language: Gothic, Baroque, Georgian, and the rest. An architect working under the influence of any such style was or is not conscious that he is inhibited by its discipline. He is, as it were, artistically brainwashed by it. Its image materializes to him every time from among the incoherent jumble of conditions presented at the outset of each architectural problem. He arranges the pieces with a free will but under some sort of hypnotic compulsion to fit them to the style image.

The twentieth-century movement was born out of the Victorian wreckage of historic styles. It was a vital revolutionary movement which fought to banish all styles, to leave each architect free to devise an individual statement for each problem. It promoted the concept of creative freedom, a state in which every architect would see a different vision for each different problem, a vision that was lying concealed among the particular puzzle pieces. While all architects would subscribe to the same architectural laws and ethics, every building would thus be independent and self-reliant. The world of architecture would be united by a consistency of approach but would be diversified and continuously revitalized by the free range of form-thoughts in answer to the contrary conditions of different building problems.

This ideal failed to develop in practice. Architects with powerful creative imagination did behave in accordance with ideal theory, producing a new form-thought from each different set of conditions, a new guide vision for each building. But some of these form-thoughts were so compelling when built that they mesmerized their own creators and a whole generation of other architects, predetermining the shape of each guiding vision almost before each architect started to stir the pieces of information. Whenever this happened the vision became a set picture and a new style came into general use. The set picture would remain in sharp focus for a time, views from every angle being spread by the architectural journals all over the world. But always there were some architects who resisted the new general guide vision, finding it unconvincing, and among these were makers of the next vision.

The Baroque language

The Georgian language

45

The first half of the twentieth century, while largely occupied in establishing an artistic language in terms of the new technology, also spent a lot of energy in establishing the right of the new industrialized world to invent a new style for itself. Eventually it was successful on both counts, and those who followed enjoyed the freedom and played with the language. Each new successful visual game stimulated more play, so that new visions appeared at quickening pace, and similar visions merged to form new styles. Each new style began by being, according to its lights, pure and simple. Later each became mannered, decorated, and finally sank decomposing into the background visual slum of this busy, ugly century. In short, each little new style of the twentieth century ran the course from inspiration to decadence like any of the old classic styles, but in no more than one-tenth the time.

Modern architecture now contains a bewildering variety of distinct styles, not to mention the various frivolous decorative fashions that have come and gone since the Modern Gothic of the adolescent skyscrapers. All this confusion in defiance of the early wish to create a style-free era is not, however, entirely without pattern. There have been three principal phases of modern architecture. All are fuzzy at the edges where they merge into one another, and the chronology is disordered. Nonetheless, they are distinct, and any strong work of twentieth-century architecture has its spiritual, artistic home in one of the three.

The first phase, beginning with the transitional and tentative early work, grew up in the 1920s, became strong in the thirties and was accepted as the world's architecture in the forties. For half a century it alone claimed the term 'modern architecture', although in fact it was split into two camps by the Atlantic Ocean. The European vision was the more radical, spectacular and influential. It was also the more international because it spoke in the language of the machine instead of a native vernacular, however refined. In the European or Functionalist vision, construction was expressed openly and with relish, provided it was new construction characteristic of a new industrialized era. Parts of the building were separated and displayed proudly, independently, provided they looked like mechanistic parts. The function of the interior showed externally, provided it was a function of which a

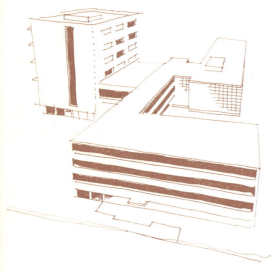

The Bauhaus at Dessau

46

brave new world could be proud. Thus fine examples of the style, including Walter Gropius's Bauhaus building at Dessau, Germany, looked as if they followed function almost literally through the motions.

The misfortune of the European Functionalist phase was that it was ahead of its time. If only computers had been available this style could have been designed by them, and it would have relished the clean coldness of the idea. The architect's job would have been the conversion of the building programme—the room sizes, their desirable juxtapositions and orientations, the available materials and the budget—into a computer programme. The computer could then have devised a planning diagram logically, rationally, at last entirely free of historic and human bias. In the absence of computers architects did their best to think as dispassionately as mathematicians.

The contemporary companion of the Functionalist was the one usually called Organic, a cosier style led and personally coloured by Frank Lloyd Wright. It had no passion for the machine. It retained a love for craftsman-wrought textures of native materials. But it was really closer in spirit to the European than was apparent on the surface. Wright, after all, was one of the early influences on the Europeans. Buildings which called themselves 'Functionalist' and those which called themselves 'Organic' were alike marked by an analytical approach to structure and to function. Both were an architecture of parts—related and composed, but separate parts.

Some serious creative buildings in the first half of the century did not conform to the analytical approach. Expressionism appeared from time to time, although mostly in paper dreams that were never realized. Erich Mendelsohn made impassioned sketches of streamlined factories. Antonio Sant'Elia was driven by the sense of power, the poetry of motion and the excitement of speed in mechanized transport. He drew projects for reshaping Italian cities in this image, and for a dream city, a 'Citta Nuova' in which skyscrapers were linked by flying bridges, elevators and multi-level roadways. Mies van der Rohe modelled tall and icy projects for glass towers. Each of these design-visions set out to express externally, if rarely internally, the human meaning of some building's function. Mies van der Rohe's search for a pure

Wright's home, Taliesin East

Sant'Elia's 'Citta Nuova' dream

47

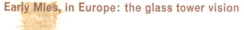

Early Mies, in Europe: the glass tower vision

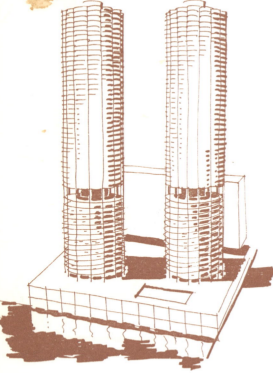

Marina City in Chicago by Bertrand Goldberg

expression of the structure and spirit of tall glass towers became a dominating influence towards the end of the first phase. Almost imperceptibly architecture turned from the analysis of parts to the incorporation of everything within a single glass box.

The glass box was as firmly devoted to the machine as early articulated Functionalist buildings were, but while those old ones spread their several parts around, expressing the various functions which were enclosed, the new attitude was to refuse recognition to minor functions and subject them to the discipline ordained by the central function. To put it more simply: in the second phase of modern architecture everything was packed into the one trunk—ideally a trunk offering such technologically-perfected shelter that any function would consider itself lucky to be packed there.

The glass box broke the spell and spirit of the first phase. Soon after, it occurred to architects that the principle could be extended beyond the austere right-angles. If the functions of an office, a school or a factory could be packed successfully into a square box, then no doubt they could be packed into boxes of more interesting shape. The right-angle represented only one branch of modern building technology: steel framing and glass sheeting. There was also concrete, and beyond it no doubt various plastics and composite materials not yet discovered, all of which might lend themselves to curves, might even be more suited to curves. So the second phase of modern architecture developed. Architects enlisted the willing assistance of engineers to build domes and twisted planes, tent shapes and giant bird shapes. Also, without troubling the engineers, architects designed for themselves cylindrical shapes and interlocking hexagonal plan shapes and octagons and a thousand and one variations of the circular plan. The second phase indeed might be symbolized by a circle.

However, the curves and the exciting shapes were not its most significant feature. This phase also claimed numerous rectilinear buildings, but these were more strictly cubic than anything in the first phase. The second phase preferred an exact square to any rectangle. In short, the second phase was a drive towards succinct, meaningful, unified or, as they said, 'significant' form. Its supporters sometimes claimed that it was also a drive back to art in architecture, implying that the first phase was anti-art, which was rarely true.

There was no clean-cut dividing line on the calendar between the phases. Splendid examples of second-phase work occur early in the history of modern architecture. Erich Mendelsohn's observatory at Potsdam, known as the Einstein Tower, was fully representative of the second phase: expressionistic, sculpturally unified, oblivious to functional and even structural reality, and it was built in 1920, more than a generation ahead of its time. Conversely, many fine examples of the first phase, expressing their functional programme in a variety of composed shapes, lingered on into the second phase and are still being built today during the third phase of twentieth-century architecture.

Having broken with Functionalism in form, the second phase warmed to the game of free design and in the work of clever and imaginative men like Philip Johnson its forms departed far from the realities of the twentieth century. It rummaged in the ruins of the past for unusual effects, not in nostalgia but in the sheer joy of playing with shapes. The second phase was embarrassingly rich in visions and styles and expressions. Its spirit ran from Mendelsohn's tower, reaching for outer space, to Saarinen's giant bird of an airport terminal forty years later, hovering forever on the verge of flight. It embraced the engineered excitement of Candela's curves and Catelano's twisted planes of concrete and the breathtaking suspended or inflated structures of Frei Otto. Its styles included the simple Monolithic, as in Saarinen's three-pointed dome at the Massachusetts Institute of Technology, and the decorated Monolithic, as in Edward D. Stone's grille-wrapped embassy at New Delhi.

No matter what the shape, the second phase was characterized by a tight unity. The buildings looked not merely all of a piece, but almost as if carved from a single piece. They were closed, final statements without prevarication, and were functionally burdened by their inflexibility and the difficulties of adding to them when the activities inside outgrew them. For this reason they were best suited to official activities uninclined to change, and to world fairs.

Whatever its faults, the second phase or second philosophical stand in modern architecture revived attention to external form

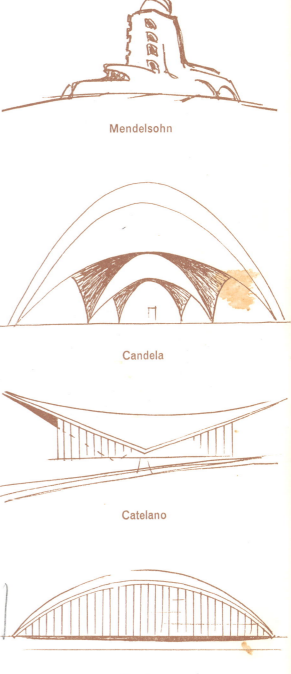

Mendelsohn

Candela

Catelano

Saarinen

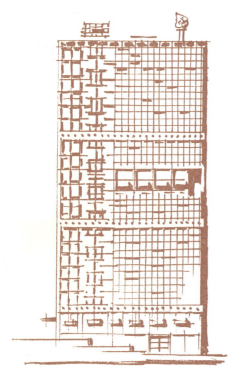

Le Corbusier project for Algiers

and reminded architects of the element of unity in design. This had been rather lacking from first-phase work, and it is essential to any building which aspires to architecture by attempting some communication of ideas. Excesses of the second phase hastened a third phase by sparking a reaction back to the 'ten-fingered grasp of reality' which Louis Sullivan sought. This third, and current, phase or philosophical stand also existed in embryo at the beginning of modern architecture. It was suggested in the less symmetrical works of Frank Lloyd Wright before 1910, in the drawings of Sant'Elia and the Futurists after World War I, and in such major prophetic works as Gropius's Tribune Tower competition entry of 1922 and Le Corbusier's skyscraper project for Algiers in 1939. The British New Brutalists contributed to it, and so did the Japanese. It is a distillation of half a century of experience in creative architecture in a technological and more or less democratic era. It is to an extent a return to the first principles of the modern movement, but it benefits from the excitement aroused in the second phase. Like the two earlier phases it is not a style, for it takes many shapes; but it has recognizable characteristics. It does not sprawl incoherently, as first-phase buildings were inclined to do, because it is too intent on conveying some formal idea, some vision of space. It is not symmetrical, as second-phase buildings were almost invariably, because it is too much alive and conscious of mundane needs like flexibility and freedom to grow, which are frustrated by a centre-line. It welcomes technological developments, but does not take them as from a grab-bag; it will be happiest when it discovers just one material from which to make an entire building. Good early buildings of the third phase, which will be examined later, like Louis Kahn's laboratories, Kenzo Tange's Yamanashi Press and Broadcasting Centre, and Paul Rudolph's architecture school at Yale, all had imitators and sparked off little styles—none more notably than the first, which in no time spawned the Random Pylon Style. But the third phase over-rode these little fashions for it was bigger than any visual effect, it was a return to a philosophical discipline. Most important, it was a return also to the understanding that architecture is an art of controlling space—not merely opening up space, or hiding a piece of it behind a space-divider, or softening the break between indoors and out-

50

doors, but a whole-hearted control of levels, volumes, and the views within and beyond. The third phase also returned to the beginning in its rejection of ornament, illusions and historic allusions.

All of the above phases and styles, which will be considered in more detail presently, at their best attempted in their own ways to achieve a state of pure architecture: a means of expression involving only architectural terms. The drama of creative architecture through the twentieth century was thus a search for a visual definition of pure architecture, and the story of architectural criticism in the same period was a search for a literary definition. Both sought a vision of architecture without pictorial, historical or sculptural associations.

If the critical search has been moderately successful, producing at least some fine florid prose and inspirational if noncommittal definitions, the search for a visual definition of pure architecture so far has been unfavoured with success. The result of this failure to find a visual image which crystallizes the splendid sentiments of the twentieth-century revolution is the anarchy, the mess we all know. Architecture is rudderless in the winds of fashion, prey to the aesthetic sirens. As a consequence most of the styles of the century were soon reduced to commercial caricatures, and eventually finished their lives in disgrace, living on only in second-rate bowling alleys and cheap motels.

In other arts such restless variety might pass without query, and the rapid changes might be stimulating to young practitioners in the medium, rather than confusing. Painting is self-rejuvenating by the process of style changes; through this century, from Cubism through symbolism and various abstractions to Pop, new ruling styles have passed at an average rate of two per generation. But the permanency of buildings and the social consequences of architectural restlessness cause architects to seek more stability, to search for an anchor, a universal theory and vision of pure building which could restore to architecture some dignity and consistency.

The vision of a completed building which an architect sees at some stage between the programming of the work and the beginning of detailed designing is his own creation, a product of his own predilections; but his predilections at any time are likely

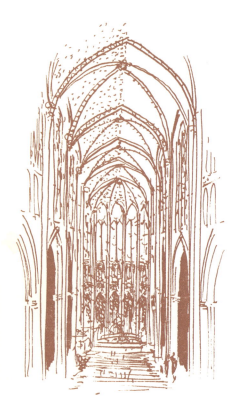

St Denis Abbey

to be shared with numerous other architects. They are likely to be epitomized in the picture of a single building that sums up brilliantly, vividly, the spirit of the age or the movement with which the architect identifies himself, in the way that the Parthenon summed up Greece. The spirit sought by the master craftsmen of the Gothic era, for instance, was contained in an image first seen in St Denis Abbey near Paris in 1144. There was something so apt in this image that within a generation it expanded and was the great cathedral of Notre Dame de Paris, to be followed soon by Bourges Cathedral and Chartres. Then it was a vision of human achievement, an inspiration in pointed arches, clustered columns and flying buttresses climbing to inaccessible vaults and lofty spires ultimately lost in the cumuli.

The epitome of a style may not be an actual building but a composite. To Brunelleschi, Leonardo, Michelangelo and other architects of the Renaissance, the guide was a composite view of Antiquity, a weighty monument of rounded arches, symmetry, classical columns, and roofs lost to sight behind stressed horizontals. The image may be of an interior space rather than an exterior mass. It may be decorative and loose rather than formal and precise, as in the Baroque period when it was crowded with angels mysteriously lit and growing brighter as they ascended to a blinding vision of Heaven itself in plaster.

Such a general image still leaves plenty of scope in most styles for individual expression and innovation. Many a great architect has been satisfied to spend his creative life within the discipline of the guide image set down for him by the society in which he lives. Of course if all were content to do this there would never be changes in architectural style, except perhaps convulsive ones after wars and revolutions when society usually demands new visions from its architects. More impetuous architects do not wait to be told. At some point in their career, normally near the beginning, an impatience with the conventions of the established image shows in their work, and by the time they are in full creative swing they are in open revolt and are building a new vision. But none of these men, however brilliant, not even Brunelleschi, Michelangelo or Frank Lloyd Wright, have created a new general style image independently or out of the blue. Michelangelo worked with intellectual security at the centre of a convention a hundred years old, and even Brunelleschi at the beginning of the Renaissance was surrounded by kindred spirits and historical precedents. Frank Lloyd Wright had Louis Sullivan behind him, and Sullivan, lonely though he was, had Richardson behind and the young Chicago school beside him. Great innovator architects may still take steps bigger than anyone else, but they do not create new styles by theory. They may be able to see one with an inner eye, but building it is another matter. This must be done gradually through successive works, each answering a particular problem in an unconventional way. The new style is the sum of all the successful departures from the previous convention.

Thus there are two guide images behind the creation of every architectural design: one general and intellectual, the other specific and artistic. The general one, whether it is traditional or revolutionary, is shared with other people—even in the case of the loneliest architect—but the specific guide vision for the building in hand, though often in fact borrowed from others, can be entirely the architect's own independent expression.

Some general guide images are almost sharp enough to obviate the need for any separate specific vision for the job in hand. Edwardian Renaissance-revival, the reigning style in many countries at the time of the twentieth-century revolution, had just such an inflexible character. Its centre-line planning and symmetrical balance of features were helpful aids to a busy architect. He used to be able to start designing almost as soon as he saw the scatter of pieces in the brief. The first move was a pencil line ruled by set-square vertically down the middle of the drawing board. The largest elements, the big rooms, were strung centrally on this, the smaller rooms added one by one on alternate sides. Finally a portico was stuck on the centre front.

The twentieth-century movement removed this first direction line for wandering designers, for it denounced symmetry, as well as ornament and pitched roofs, with the zeal of Rationalist missionaries attacking icons.

At the beginning, long before it found expression in buildings, modern architecture had no form and little enough to do with practical design. It was an intellectual idea, and one which escaped the few attempts to build it into brick and mortar. It was

Guaranty Building by Sullivan, 1894

one of the revolutionary architectural theories which heaved occasionally under the ornate surface of nineteenth-century building. At first the theory was necessarily destructive, denouncing all smug imitations of the past, calling for freedom from ancient habits of building and the now irrelevant rules of historic styles. The revolution stirred in Central Europe and in the Middle West of the U.S.A. at first nothing much but words. Then it became constructive and a vision formed—and became two: one in each continent. The movement that was represented by the skyscrapers of Louis Sullivan and others in Chicago in the 1880s and 1890s, and the 'prairie houses' of Frank Lloyd Wright around the turn of the century, was akin to its contemporary European movement mainly in that both were in revolt against the past. The Chicago school faded early in the twentieth century, though Frank Lloyd Wright continued until 1959 in his own independent, inimitable and fairly uncommunicable way. The European movement was impressed and stirred by Wright's early adventures but not really diverted from its own course, and by the 1920s, under the guidance of men like Walter Gropius, it had formulated its radical style of austere simplicity and was beginning to feel its strength. Then World War I broke out and all but destroyed it.

In Chicago's revolt against the past there was still some room for romance. Louis Sullivan never could resist ornament and Frank Lloyd Wright never could see any reason why he should attempt to resist it. But the romantic approach went far deeper than the surface. Wright's guide visions were always to some extent idealistic, while in the European revolution romance and idealism of any sort were considered as decadent and indefensible as symmetry. There, the new moral anchor for architects was the idea of realism: buildings which are what they are, and look it; architecture for living, pure and simple; architecture spared the indignity of any sort of applied art and uncontaminated even by the desire for beauty.

In practical application this idea of realism had to split into two —as is always necessary in architecture where form and surface are almost independent elements. Thus the new rule for form was to follow function, as Sullivan had stated it, or as an earlier American, Horatio Greenough, had said in 1851: 'unflinching adaptation to position and use'. As for ornament, the new European rule was to banish it entirely, since it was clearly no more flattering to an advanced civilization than the slashes of warpaint on a savage's skin, as Adolf Loos remarked. To many revolutionaries the spirit of democracy and the nature of technology sent up an irrestible call for a new, entirely rational approach to all building design. The resulting buildings were unique in history, not only because they allowed themselves to be shaped by the demands of new materials like reinforced concrete and glass, but also because they were deliberately unornamented. While often being far removed from the utilitarian, they delighted in the look of utility, or better still, suitability. They wanted realism in the interpretation of the needs of the people they were sheltering. They abhorred fake. They did their utmost to be reasonable and rational.

Try to imagine the mood of architects carrying these new principles from a stuffy Victorian parlour into a clean new century —free at last, they imagined, of the suffocating dictatorship of historic rules. Naturally they reacted violently against the old styles, and especially against the grotesque forms, the parodies of historical shapes, the ornamental confusion on the surface of the past fifty years. Naturally their new concept of rational simplicity led to the placing of bricks, concrete, glass and steel in the simplest of geometrical forms. The anti-ornament ethics led to an absolute plainness of solid blocks, exposed steel frames, and walls of glass, in rectilinear boxes with no visible roofs.

The principle of allowing the structure freely to suggest the shape led to minor acrobatic feats like cantilevers and corner windows. Distaste for the old order led to various gestures of independence from the Greeks, such as deliberate effects of unbalance: weight poised over void, gashes for windows where least expected, and so on. Everything was done in the name of rationalism, realism and Functionalism, and while the results were usually intensely genuine and often rawly sensitive, they were still no more than artistic expressions of these principles, and this was art performed in a heady mood of rebellion.

The European movement had many subdivisions including de Stijl group of Holland, Futurism in Italy, and Constructivism as in early Russian revolutionary days. The most influential and persistent of all was that which centred on the Bauhaus of Germany.

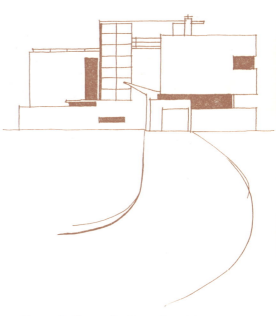

House in Surrey by Connell and Ward, 1932

The Fagus factory

In the early years of this century, when the growth of industry was still in practically direct proportion to the growth of ugliness, when mechanization meant to most people the very antithesis of all that was meant by the word art, Walter Gropius saw the futility of fighting the machine. Under him, the Bauhaus taught that the artist and the engineer and the technician must be brought together to work in mutual respect and understanding. The Bauhaus, in teaching the essential unity of all the visual arts, and in preaching collaboration, sought in effect to subdue the personal vision. The Bauhaus encouraged artists out of their garrets to work in the machine shops of the modern world with as many collaborators of kindred feeling as they could bear to mix with. The Bauhaus trained artists who were technicians, and technical men who were artists.

Gropius's first building, designed after he opened his own practice in 1910, aged twenty-seven, brilliantly epitomized the central European movement. It was the Fagus works at Alfeld an der Leine, an extraordinarily prophetical building with its walls of glass in steel stretched over the open framework like cellophane over a wire cage. It became a general guide vision for the generation of *avant-garde* architects which was then at the impressionable age.

In the simplest terms, the Bauhaus's architectural philosophy was that everything that man makes should follow nature's rules and derive its form from the demands of its function and the character of the materials used. To achieve this, art and technique had to be fused into one, which meant that artists were best trained in the workshop, gaining familiarity with machines and materials.

The original teaching of the Bauhaus could seldom be accused of artiness, even on the most sophisticated plane, for the work was anchored to reality by impressing on the student the moral obligation to be useful to the community. But the atmosphere of stimulating adventure into new forms of expression which permeated its studios did not carry well beyond them. What carried best was the image of a machine-made product: hard, sharp, metallic; nothing crafted or built up painfully of little pieces, but something stamped out by an enormous mechanism in one or two irrevocable and miraculously intermeshed movements.

In 1925 when the Bauhaus moved to Dessau, this image took form more concrete and impressive than ever before in the new building group which Walter Gropius designed for it. The Dessau Bauhaus carried the Fagus character further. Its shape was developed freely from the functional requirements. The plan expanded, giving separate emphasis and form to the various parts. It had three uneven wings: two storeys in height where necessary, four storeys for the main workshops, six storeys for the students' studio-dormitories. Where light was essential, a glass skin even more fragile and detached in appearance than the one used in the Fagus building was drawn over the concrete frame. In other parts strip windows were more suitable, so solid bands were hung on the outer skin between the strips of glass. In the dormitory block, balconies broke the wall. This epochal design, owing almost nothing to past styles, was a triumph for the machine look. Each significant requirement of accommodation as set out in the building program could be seen: independently recognized, considered, solved. For this reason, design which followed the Bauhaus example was called, in due course, Programmatic Functionalism.

The unmatched but related wings suggested the working parts of a giant machine made for teaching design. For the first time in serious architecture, the ancient rule of unity in art was deliberately broken. The Bauhaus building was not one thing. It was several things. Nevertheless, these things were composed and controlled. The principle of separation and articulation might easily have led to fussiness, but this was not permitted. There was nothing in the principle, for instance, to restrain the exterior from expressing the separate internal functions of the bathrooms, the storage spaces, or other such essential if small elements of the accommodation. But these things were not articulated; they were subordinated, thanks to Walter Gropius's personal and excellent sense of scale. The parts that he promoted to separate expression were big enough and meaningful enough to have been significant little buildings in their own right.

The Bauhaus building at Dessau crystallized machine aesthetics in architectural terms. It became the next general guide vision for the modern world. For twenty years the articulation of building parts was the principle which ruled design conceptions by most

The Bauhaus at Dessau

57

progressive architects in most countries. The scale of the elements selected for separation and individual expression were in the order of the scale adopted by Gropius. It was a convincing and convenient way of design and its great international success was partly due to its freedom from reliance on artistic talent. The most pedestrian mind could be taught to design competently in machine aesthetics, or Programmatic Functionalism, or—as it later came to be known—the International Style.

Eventually architects grew tired of the plain surfaces and articulated forms, and they counter-revolted not only against the appearance but also against the principles involved. Long before the general counter-revolution of the 1950s, which we shall examine later, there were minor skirmishes on the sidelines. The first of these occurred immediately after World War I.

There had to be some temporary reaction to the idea of rational simplicity, even in serious architectural circles, after the misery and austerity of the war. It took the form of an Expressionism which was closer to sculpture than architecture. Referring again to the famous example of Erich Mendelsohn's Einstein Tower, this observatory building served a function which might have been expected to evoke the most rational and scientifically bald solution. Instead, Mendelsohn chose for a guide an image expressing by external sculptural means the spirit of scientific investigation, or at any rate movement forward, of aspiration to the stars, or at any rate a reaching upwards. In development of the form he curved the windows illogically and was not deterred when for economic reasons he could not make it in the concrete for which it was obviously designed. He made it of brick, plastered. It was a stunning, exciting building which denied almost every principle of good architecture, like Spanish Baroque.

Twentieth-century architecture soon recovered from this first Expressionist deviation. By the mid-1920s the International Style was established in Central Europe and Holland. In 1930 it was adopted by Sweden. It picked up wood there, and travelled on. It made appearances in England and the U.S.A. late in the 1920s, but only very tentatively. It grew stronger in England in the early thirties. No house in the world sums up the anonymous aesthetic of the whole period before World War II better than Serge Chermayeff's little plastered butterbox built at Rugby in 1933. This was

Mendelsohn's Einstein Tower

58

a cube interrupted only by a sun balcony, a single circular cantilever at one corner thrust boldly out into the pale sun. By 1934 the
new architecture was appearing in the West Coast of America
and in Australia. By World War II it was all round the world, but
meanwhile had been banned by Hitler in the countries of its
infancy, and by Stalin in Russia. After the war, outside the area of
Stalin's influence, the International Style of architecture was
universal.

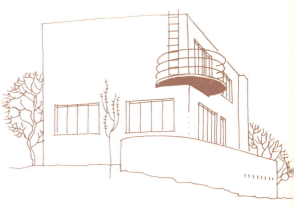

Chermayeff's house at Rugby

Yet all this time Frank Lloyd Wright was continuing to build in
Chicago and other parts of the U.S.A., and sometimes abroad.
He was not building on the scale that he would have liked to be,
but nevertheless he was constantly working, designing or writing,
and influencing others. He built mainly houses, churches, and
other intimate buildings for the cosier human functions, for his
work attracted clients with problems in this category rather than
—with notable exceptions—industrialists or investors. In 1932, the
year that Henry-Russell Hitchcock and Philip Johnson introduced
the European movement to the American public in an exhibition
called 'The International Style' at New York's Museum of Modern
Art, Wright was a thoroughly mature designer in his own uniquely
independent style. He called his work modern architecture, but
the examples of European modern architecture displayed at the
Museum of Modern Art were as foreign to him as the classical
revivals from which he had broken free a generation earlier. He
had nothing in common with it, and he damned it and ridiculed its
practitioners till the day he died. He called it inhuman, undemo-
cratic and, more accurately but with a strangely bitter paro-
chialism, un-American. In his belief it worshipped technology and
neglected the poor human beings who were obliged to occupy it
He considered, fairly enough, that his own designs exploited
technology in the service of the human beings sheltered. He called
his way Organic, and the other way an affront to humanity, not
really preferable to the Victorian revivals.

Thus when World War II was over the twentieth-century movement could not present to young architects or fanciers of the art
a single, coherent general vision to guide the way ahead. It presented two guide images. One was a direct development from
Europe's white boxes of the early thirties. The box was made now
of more practical materials more likely to stay white, and perhaps

59

its walls now had larger areas of unbroken glass. It was, however, still essentially and proudly representative of the International Style. Not that its supporters liked that name. They called it simply modern architecture, or, if pressed to be more precise, Functionalist. Others called it variously Rationalist, Diagrammatic, Geometrical, Cubist, Mechanistic, and so on. The other general guide vision presented by twentieth-century architecture at its half-way mark in 1950 was influenced by Frank Lloyd Wright, but it was a by-product of his humanist attitude rather than his personal style. At this time Wright's own style was too difficult for workaday architects to assume. It could be watered down quite successfully, however, by injecting Wrightian flavours—something of the warmth of his preferred surface treatments of wood, stone, and rusty autumn colours—into the cold rectilinear geometry of the European form. This branch of the movement was inclined to call itself Organic. Wherever it was practised it took on something of local characteristics, mainly because of the use of local materials. In San Francisco it was called Bay Region Style. In Sweden, where it also picked up a few modest traditional decorative devices it attracted the name New Empiricism. In small areas of Australia where it prospered, as on parts of the Mornington Peninsula, Victoria, it took up chameleon-like colour again and deluded some observers into thinking it had inherent indigenous qualities. More objective critics called it Romantic, and its harsher detractors dismissed it as sentimental Cottage Style.

The machine and the cottage, different though they were, had more in common than either had with any earlier style. Apart from certain ethical rules governing one's attitude to function and structure they had in common an attitude to space—the space enclosed by the building—which was new, a by-product perhaps of twentieth-century astronomy and even of moving pictures. For the new concept of space depended upon changes and surprise, on the different aspects of any object, any enclosure, which reveal themselves as an observer, like a roving movie camera, passes round a room, up a stairway, leans over a balustrade and looks down, or up, to further floors; as he moves from cramped quarters to a great open hall; as he sees a suggestion of an extension of his enclosure around or over a screen, and on moving finds more of this prospect revealed; even as he experiences

Organic Cottage Style

60

vertigo at a drop. Twentieth-century space is asymmetrical, teasing, promising, endless.

For instance, an observer rises to a mezzanine balcony within a large hall, or living-room. His view of the hall itself has altered. Moreover he can see above a half-height screen on the other side to an extension of the enclosure through glass to a terrace of the same width, then on to the horizon. But what else lies behind the screen? The answer might be crashingly dull, but it is the architect's secret for the time being. Both machine and cottage recognized that the essence of architectural art was the atmospheric modelling of enclosed space.

This was important, but they appeared otherwise to be very different. In their overall geometry and their decorative qualities they were poles apart. Thus there developed a twentieth-century 'Battle of the Styles', as hotly contested as the Classical v. Gothic battle of the nineteenth century. While the two new styles were by no means confined to residential architecture, the opposing positions were best represented by two house images. One was the white plaster box such as Chermeyeff built at Rugby, clearly a proud man-made thing almost oblivious to its environment, unchanging whether built in England or Chicago or in the yard of the Museum of Modern Art, and outraged if trees or creepers were allowed close enough to interrupt the geometrical precision. The other house image was best represented by Frank Lloyd Wright's Robie house of 1906 in Chicago, with its wide eaves and low gabled roof spreading horizontal layers above deep-shaded cosy retreats, a house not at home until in a garden, encouraging shrubs in flower boxes, and creepers on pergolas, and loungers on terraces.

Each of these two house-images represented one fork of the crossroads at which twentieth-century architecture, half-grown, stood in 1950, hesitating. It had fought its revolution against traditional forms and won, and was accepted everywhere. The world war was over, and building industry was on the brink of unparalleled activity. But many a young architect on the threshold of his career was lost between the images. He was likely to be attracted to either, depending on circumstances, while he noted the dangers of artificiality with one and of sentimentality with the other. Names confused the issue. It may have been true that the

Wright's Robie house

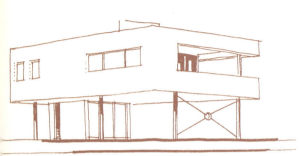

Wright/cottage image was more organic, regionalist and even empirical than the Gropius/mechanistic image, but it was by no means necessarily more romantic. The European crystal prism for living was romantic, despite protestations. Nor was the cottage image always less rational. For one thing, its stress of horizontals and low, long lines brought it in close contact with the ground and made for the easy access between indoors and outdoors which is fairly essential to good living, notwithstanding the jokes at its expense. The machine-made butterbox which was nominally Functionalist, on the contrary, often used to climb on stilts high above the ground. This was justified in argument, sometimes rather unconvincingly, on the grounds that the covered space thus created at ground level allowed for car-parking. Also the view was better at the higher level. But there was really no disguising the fact that the stilts were climbed in a gesture of defiance against traditional forms of earthbound construction. The illusion of levitation was enjoyable in itself. Yet the butterbox, in other ways, in its selection and use of materials, in its precision and sterility, was clearly facing tomorrow, while in many of its somewhat nostalgic effects the cottage was looking over its shoulder.

About this time, in the 1949 edition of a most influential book, *Space, Time and Architecture*, Dr Sigfried Giedion wrote of the contrast between Organic and Geometrical Styles throughout history, and he remarked that 'the artist has the right of choice, of saying according to his own point of view which pleases him and which he will follow'. He assumed, as did most observers of the divergent schools of thought, that the forks of this crossroad were spread so widely that there could be no bridge between them. At the best a rare genius like Alvar Aalto, the clever Finn, may be able to pick out a narrow track, apparent to no one else, through the swamp between. Giedion and other writers, in presenting the artistic choice to the young architect, implied that any decision he made would be binding for life. Any architect who attempted to walk with one foot on each road, who would dream of jumping occasionally from one road to the other, was as far beneath contempt as a nineteenth-century eclectic ready to change from Gothic to Scottish Baronial at the drop of a hat, and as surely doomed to fall into ridicule. The suggestion of irrevocability in the making of the choice was unnerving to young architects, but these were the last days of belief in the infallibility of the revolution.

In March 1950 an editor of the *Architectural Review* of London, the historian-critic J. M. Richards, in an important article, surveyed the growing disenchantment with Functionalist dogma and pointed to 'the logical next step, the Functionalism of the particular'.

'There is', Richards wrote, 'no call to abandon Functionalism.' He suggested on the contrary that design should relate ever more closely to 'the essential particulars of time and place and purpose'. This statement at the half-century mark suggested a helpful philosophy to the puzzled young man. It indicated a general desire at the time to see the divergent roads draw together, to tidy up the architectural scene by rallying everyone under a common flag. There were other calls, and responses, to positive kinds of compromises between the schools. It seemed then that the eventual absorption of the opposing schools in a single central movement—at last really infallible—was possible and indeed inevitable.

This desire for a tidying-up of differences in modern architecture and consolidation in a single image was mainly confined to those who had identified themselves in some way with the European revolution of twentieth-century design in the early years. They could not bear to see the principles which had inflamed a generation go astray. And it could be pointed out that the differences between the butterbox and the cottage were in many instances quite superficial and unimportant. The cottage school, for instance, was fond of the character of timber, and delighted in any piece with a pronounced grain, leaving it unsullied by any paint or varnish. The butterbox used timber too, but underneath a coat of paint. It was less fascinated by the wood than by the machine which cut and planed it. The two images were poles apart aesthetically but they were both strong and valid expressions of the times in which they were built.

The visual discrepancies between the two schools were in fact less important than the mutual aims.

Each expressed its structure, though in rather different ways. The cottage exposed its timber posts, beams and rafters. The

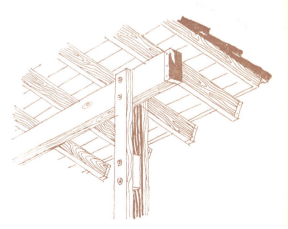

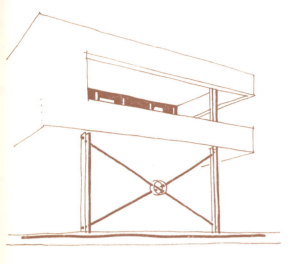

butterbox was not especially interested in such details of humble carpentry but revelled in the feeling of suspended rigidity and was prouder to expose cross-bracing between the stilts on which it floated.

Each was dedicated to the new concept of promising, teasing space; their plans developed internal spatial effects, merging internal rooms and carrying them outdoors through walls of glass.

Each was intent on creating artistic unity, though the butterbox did this by means of clean-cut external form, or a linked series of succinct clean-cut forms, while the cottage sought unity through the composition of visually compatible parts.

The differences could all be reduced to aesthetic rather than ideological matters. Even the most obvious difference—the cosy complexity of the cottage against the bald sterility of the butter-box—was largely a matter of scale. Both believed in simplicity, but whereas the butterbox held that simplicity was best served by a flush sheet which concealed the complexity, the cottage held that fundamental simplicity was achieved only when all the structure was exposed. In fact most subscribers to each school of thought agreed to expose the large elements of reinforced concrete framing and most seemed to agree to conceal the smaller elements of timber wall framing.

In 1950 another solution to the split image of modern architecture seemed possible, and more potentially exciting than a compromise. This was suggested by Dr Giedion. His earlier rather disciplinarian attitude was now modified. In the February issue of the *Architectural Review* he wrote of the need for architects 'to leap from the rational-functional to the irrational-organic'. The suggestion now was that it would not indicate weakness to admit the possibility of the two roads of modern architecture continuing their separate ways, even increasing the divergence and therefore the scale of architectural quality that bridged them. An architect might feel free to draw upon different parts of this scale according to the emotional impulse of the occasion. It was true that the work of some architects of the early 1950s indicated the possibility of competent buildings in both schools being produced by one man. It seemed possible that architecture might develop the atmospheric scale between the two extremes.

Then an architect could select the mood along the scale that best suited the conditions, place and purpose of his building, as other artists in other fields determine the key or the tempo for the case. The two general guide visions would be dissolved into each other and their sharp focus lost. More artistic responsibility would devolve upon the architect. He would enjoy, for example, something of the freedom of expression, of change of mood, which permitted the author of *Man and Superman* to write *Saint Joan*.

For the butterbox and the cottage, the European and the American, the Functionalist and the Organic, were not as incompatible as they looked. No conflicting theories of any real significance lay behind them. They had similar roots. Both grew out of disgust with the Victorian era's shallow copies of historic styles. There was really little more than the difference of mood which attended their conceptions. The smallest adjustment of the architect's outlook, stimulated by a fine afternoon or depressed by a neighboring eyesore, might be sufficient to change the key to which all materials and details were tuned. Before 1950 there had been a certain restraint against change on every architect who once set his foot on either road. To have switched to the other side would have indicated a weakening of resolve and lack of decision. But so long as the architect retained the aspiration of discovering the truth of building, so long as he was dedicated to the human being and to ultimate simplicity of means, surely he could be allowed an occasional change of mood?

Thus, despite some ideological arguments between the two sides of modern architecture, at the middle of the century compromises and gentle bridges between the two could be contemplated, because practically all serious architects at the time had in common a belief in functional design. While the European school of the butterbox was more often called Functionalist, sometimes in a rather sneering tone, the American cottage school claimed that it was the truly functional style. Its grandfather, Louis Sullivan, was after all the man who coined the famous phrase, 'form follows function'. The cottage form, the typical Organic plan, spread its wings freely in answer to functional requirements, and its architects criticized the Europeans' stricter, more inhibiting geometry precisely because it was not functional. The European school answered this by explaining that its values were broader and more rational than intimate needs of a particular problem. It was seeking universal answers to functional and structural problems of our age. When Mies van der Rohe stated baldly his disagreement with the almost sacrosanct Sullivan phrase, and reversed it, proclaiming that his aim was to build pure universal form which function would have to follow, he was not denouncing Functionalism. He was merely criticizing the idea of structural and artistic individuality in the age of technology. The pioneers' concept that every element of every building required a functional justification was never questioned by serious architects of this time. (It should not be necessary to mention that serious architects are always in a minority in the building industry in any country, so that the domination of non-functioning elements was never really threatened outside the pages of the architectural press.) Nevertheless, in serious architectural circles a fair degree of unanimity and a display of solidarity could be mustered at the half century, and Philip Johnson was able to say in 1951: 'With the mid-century, modern architecture has come of age.'

The coming of age was celebrated, as it were, by the United Nations Secretariat building, a machine in a box expanded into the most enormous glass-sided slab standing forty storeys beside New York's East River. It was designed by a team of half a dozen architects from member nations of the United Nations. One of them was Le Corbusier, who contributed the guide picture in the form of a scribble on tissue paper but never forgave the way this was interpreted by Wallace Harrison, the United States representative and team-leader. The finished Secretariat exemplified an international approach and teamwork, as opposed to the Wright kind of introverted genius. In its size and elegant slimness it represented the full maturity, the highest development, of the butterbox. It was a direct descendant of some of the earliest pioneering buildings of the century. Essentially it was built to the guide vision created by Gropius in the Fagus factory in 1911. The United Nations Secretariat had the same approach, the same principles, the same aesthetic impulse. All the earlier boxes suddenly looked tentative. This plain slab

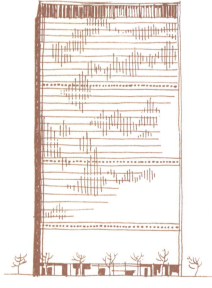

United Nations Secretariat

was, except for a few minor imperfections, the ultimate rectilinear form. It was one image, unadorned, windowless (while being all window). It was a monument to technology and impersonal architectural technique. It was a strong statement in a language which the ordinary busy architect could easily adopt. It was a guide vision for the poor professional designer as unequivocal and helpful as the centralized symmetry of Victorian Renaissance. It seemed to represent the end of a search for form begun in the Fagus building. Modern architecture had arrived at a goal dimly outlined fifty years earlier. It had also arrived at a crisis.

In fact the same straight road did go on a little further. Or rather it broadened out into a turning circle at the end. Workaday architects all over the world took the curtain wall from United Nations. At first they made faithful copies, but very soon they began making minor adjustments to justify their fees and their self-respect. Often they tried to improve the plain metal or glass panels between the clear windows with brighter colour, or folds, or pressed patterns of more complexity. Generally they monkeyed about within the established formulae. They were marking time at the end of the road, as it were, until some leader would arrive and give them new instructions. However, one or two sensitive designers pushed on a little further beyond the United Nations, or at any rate widened the turning circle. Skidmore, Owings and Merrill gave the glass box new life by dividing it and hollowing part of it to make Lever House in Park Avenue; they put a square doughnut base below a little United Nations slab. Pedestrians passing by and under the doughnut could look up through its hole to the tall slab poised above. Thus something of the essential spatial element of architecture was added at the base, while the box above remained a pure technological machine. Later, across Park Avenue in the Seagram Building, Mies van der Rohe added some further surface polish to the box, simplifying its skin till it was nothing but an elegantly, classically proportioned bronze grid holding sheets of bronze-tinted glass. Now it seemed certain that the end of the road was reached. Any further simplification seemed unlikely, at least until someone invented a new sort of material—fireproof, continuous, transparent—which would eliminate even the simplest metal framework.

The atmosphere at the end of the road may have suited Mies

The Seagram Building

van der Rohe, who had plotted out the journey years earlier in Europe and had led thousands of others all the way. It may have suited busy commercial architects who now had the simplest guide picture in history and were able to convert it into a complete, clean, smart design by consulting a catalogue of curtain walling patterns. But it did not suit many men of taste, who were dissatisfied with the banal box for nostalgic and sometimes other better reasons; and it did not suit the small proportion of architects who considered their calling to be primarily a creative art. It held the interest of the ordinary man in the street only briefly while the novelty lasted. The International Style, after a whole generation of struggle, went to the top of a wave of fashion and down on the other side in a matter of months. As quickly as plainness gained a fashionable lift, it lost it again. Among architects, the Functionalist theory still commanded some respect, but little enthusiasm. A glimmer of the old joy of invention accompanied early technological developments of the curtain wall, and there were moments of revived visual delight when it was discovered that the glass curtain, although in itself as clean and innocent as could be, reflected in engaging distortions the clouds and any quaint old buildings that happened to be opposite. These attractions also faded fairly quickly.

Soon after Lever House and long before 1957 when the Seagram Building was finished, many architects were growing dissatisfied with the cube, the right-angle, the glass wall and the plain surface—dissatisfied with the machine. The glass wall had passed from the mind of the architectural artist over to the hands of the building technologist, and now the restless creators of the profession set out to find something more personal. They wanted to make architecture an expressive art again. If in the process all the rational theory of the first half of the century had to be thrown overboard, then overboard it must go. 'They left the safe anchorage of functionality, technology and anonymous teamwork to start the long voyage home to architecture as art.' So wrote Sibyl Moholy-Nagy in 1964 of the men who learnt and revered the Bauhaus doctrine at Harvard but then seemed to rebel against it as soon as they had a chance to build. Professor Moholy-Nagy, like most critics and observers, apparently assumed that the Bauhaus code would have to be broken down point by point in order to let art grow, until there would be nothing left of it. Others, who still believed in early twentieth-century revolutionary theory, hoped that a way could be found to restore architecture to the company of the fine arts without demolishing that theory, without tearing down the Bauhaus flag, without denying the rational code and the realist aim of building.

The search for a new direction meant firstly a tracking back some way over one's own paces to find a suitable place from which one might branch off, to see where the main development got too set in its ways. Even something already dismissed, like the cottage vision, demanded reassessment.

Frank Lloyd Wright had always disparaged the soulless box. Perhaps his was the correct and the only way after all? But this was not good enough in the 1950s. A retreat to the cottage aesthetic did not suit the searching spirit of the new architectural adventurers. An affluent post-war decade unquestionably called for a new approach, a new spirit of abundance in architecture. The austerity of the International Style may have been meaningful and refreshing after a surfeit of ornamentation, but now it seemed only a restrictive bore. To the great majority of practising architects all over the world, poised on the threshold of a new area promising unprecedented technological adventures, it seemed that the time had come to reassess, and perhaps to reject, the restricting principle of Functionalism. And yet, strangely enough, the idea of rejection was not easy to accept. Functionalism had for modern architecture more than merely sentimental attraction. Functionalism was bound up with the whole of twentieth century design, morally and inspirationally. Now in the 1950s most vital members of the modern movement wanted to renounce Functionalism, and yet were torn by remorse and doubt at the thought, for they had no other conviction to replace this guiding light of their youth.

Whenever architects at this time were tempted to build from the heart and not from the head they had the uneasy feeling that they were somehow letting the old side down. The single-minded revolutionary zeal of the early years was gone, and yet there was nothing in its place but a half-smug and half-dispirited slackening of the discipline. If there had been a new god there would have been no hesitation, but in place of ideals there were only reactions. These worked against simplicity and direct statements, and most of them were explained or excused with somewhat sentimental arguments which called for a revival of more 'human' qualities, in terms which frequently sounded more like advertisements for Coca-Cola. Serious architects who questioned the old law of Functionalism were in danger of finding themselves in the same camp as the interior decorators and the home magazines. They were mixed up. Yet perhaps their doubts and confusion were not entirely due to a sudden weakening of resolve in this generation. Despite the brilliance and the bravery of the pioneers of twentieth-century architecture, their original movement lacked a clear goal. The principle of design-for-function was presented too often as if it were a style or character of building and an end in itself. It was none of these things. Functionalism was an ethical rule and a technique of design, not some sort of mood or atmosphere. It was not something to be set up in opposition to the genre of humanistic design. It could never be a substitute for creative architectural thought. Functionalism is, as it were, the mould in which good architecture is cast, rather than an ingredient. As a technique and a philosophical basis for design, Functionalism still held in the fifties the promise to direct and unite all the useful arts. It was a minor tragedy of twentieth-century civilization that this unique artistic idea began to die before it was properly tested, while still young and inexperienced. It was discarded by the *avant-garde* while virtually only one application of its principles, the articulated machine, had been investigated with any thoroughness or conscientiousness, and even this one application was still so unfamiliar in the streets of most countries that the layman had not had sufficient opportunity to adjust to it and evaluate it. Functionalism was renounced at this time, almost guiltily at first but with growing confidence, because the first attempts to apply the principle of functional ethics always tended in the same direction, and it was not visually an exciting direction.

Eager, creative men grew tired of Functionalism; but its philosophical basis, which has some spark of eternal truth and validity, is bigger than any one of its possible applications. It is no less than Nature's way of designing, although the parallel may not be immediately apparent if one compares, say, the traditional functionally designed dog-kennel and its inmate. The former is certainly honest, but a thought too crude. The latter is frequently beautiful. A Functionalist could not design a dog (not even a toy dog if he is devout). However, this is not because he would be working from wrong principles, but only because his brain could not stretch to absorb the immense complexity and number of puzzle pieces related to the design problem of a dog, even if some computer could list half of them for him. But if we narrow the dog design problem down, and take a simple bit like the tail, then the Functionalist could understand most of the problems and could start work at the drawing board, and would doubtless design almost the same structural shape as Nature designs, even if he couldn't get it to wag. Microscopic examination of natural structure in bones, trees, leaves and so on usually reveals an architectonic pattern: ordered, rhythmic, consistent, balanced, thoroughly understandable to second-year engineering students, Nature can be as crude as the dog kennel when her problem is as simple as that, which it frequently is at microscopic scale. Yet even then she is varied, whereas only one application of Functionalism suggested itself to men who were in open revolution against the aimless anarchy of nineteenth-century eclectic exhibitionism. They saw a line of development which started with a white cube of concrete and appeared to lead to a green cube of glass. By the mid-1950s this line had been traversed assiduously, and some architects, finding the end result lacking in atmospherics, and not patient enough to enquire if other possibilities had been investigated along the line, were at this time all for throwing out the infant principles of Functionalism along with the bathwater of the glass cubes.

Two houses of the time were the centre of much ideological argument. One was by Mies van der Rohe, designed in 1946 and built in 1950 for Dr Edith Farnsworth among big trees in a field near Chicago. The other was built by Philip Johnson for himself on a hillside at New Canaan, Connecticut, in 1949. They were the two most elegant glass boxes ever built and critics spent many words explaining their subtle differences. The concept and plan of each house made the simplest of earlier butterboxes look complicated. Their simplicity was much more impressive than that of the contemporary United Nations Secretariat, for at heart

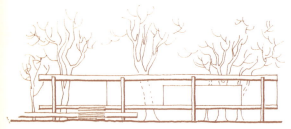

Mies's Farnsworth house

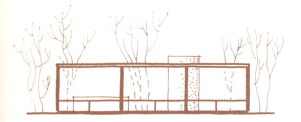

Johnson's Johnson house

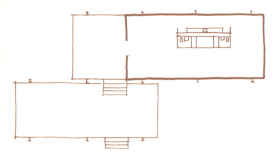

Farnsworth house plan

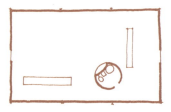

Johnson house plan

inside its glass skin the United Nations was a conventionally complicated office building. In these two transparent houses the simplicity extended right through the glass wall and out the other side. In each case the plan was a rectangle, with glass walls all round. Only the bathroom was made private behind solid walls dropped off-centre into the plan—shaped as another rectangle in the Farnsworth house, as a circle in the Johnson house. All the rest of the house—living, cooking, sleeping areas—was an open space barely screened from the weather and the woods by the walls of plate glass held in smooth polished steel staunchions. The Farnsworth house was elevated just above the grass and its underside was a beautifully finished smooth surface which would be seen by no one except pet animals or children after a lost ball. The Johnson house sat on the lawn. In each case the strength and purity of form and detail in the scheme was so intense that few who studied it were left unmoved. Many architects and prominent architectural journals regarded both with reverence, not indeed as practical prototypes for democratic family houses, but as unique pavilions and as exercises in perfection of an idea: the glass box idea. Yet the difference between the detached professional intellectual view and the layman's subjective practical one was never more pronounced. Non-architects, observing these glass cages, imagined themselves living inside, displayed like goldfish to anyone wandering by, as they shivered or roasted according to the season.

Mies van der Rohe was of course the master, one of the first generation of modern architecture, and Philip Johnson was his pupil, or disciple. Mies designed his glass house first and gave this guide picture, as it were, to Johnson. Mies's project proceeded slowly and the less-elaborately simple Johnson house was finished about a year earlier. Several commentators immediately perceived a most important academic or stylistic difference between these two sister glass boxes. The Farnsworth house, by the older man, Mies, was still a modern house in the early European twentieth-century tradition. It had the old revolutionary anti-gravity gestures of the raised floor and cantilever ends. It was still articulated to some extent, in that the outdoor living platform was separate and deliberately placed out of line from the box itself. The Johnson house on the contrary suggested a tentative move to a new solution to the ancient puzzle. This was the opposite from articulation. It was a move back to coherent form, to a more intense concentration on the old artistic principle of unity. The Farnsworth house carried the International Style's concept of simplicity practically to the end of the road. It concluded one investigation. The Johnson house opened another, extending the idea of simplicity into visual oneness. Its spare steel frame was painted black so that it was inclined to dissolve into the dark reflections in the glass it held. Its roof was a tight lid trimmed to the line of the glass on all sides. It was one thing to see, pure and simple, and it led to the monolithic vision which we shall examine in more detail presently. It is true that Philip Johnson had to build another pavilion nearby to make the glass house work. This was a guest-wing of bedrooms decently withdrawn inside brick walls. He made it visually complementary to the glass house, so far as possible a negative version of the same thing, but he did not allow it to come close enough down the garden path which separated them to disturb the clear entity of the glass house.

Frank Lloyd Wright met Philip Johnson at a function some time later and greeted him: 'Hello, Philip. Are you still putting up little houses and leaving them out in the rain?' This remark expressed the incompatibility of the two visions as tartly as Johnson's description of Wright as the greatest architect of the nineteenth century. Wright, the roof lover, had a democratic majority on his side in this division, for most non-architects are, by conditioning, lovers of sheltering, comforting, overhanging roofs. The Johnson and Farnsworth houses seemed so impractical to most laymen that few were interested in considering them seriously on artistic grounds. The Farnsworth house was regarded as morally dubious as well, since Mies had wished this glass cage on a client while Johnson at least was building only for himself. Yet the importance of the two houses lay to a great extent on the very fact that they had driven earlier solutions to the illogical conclusion. They were done so superbly in their subtly different ways as to be the final words on the subject of glass houses. After these pure boxes no one could have expected the International Style to hold further undiscovered artistic secrets of any significance.

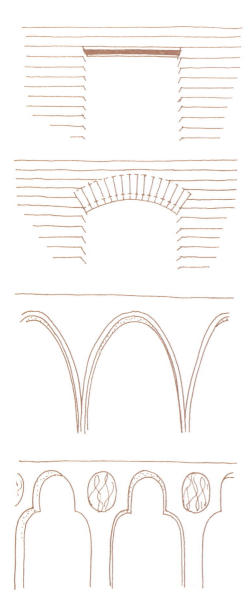

Led by Mies and by the United Nations building, as we have seen, the world was now adopting the glass box as a universal guide solution. However, in the eyes of the architectural *avant-garde*, that line of investigation was closed. If this stage had been reached earlier when the Functionalist principles of the European movement were still fresh, then other applications of those principles might have appeared spontaneously. More attention might have been concentrated on other means of achieving purity of form in accordance with function, in terms not necessarily limited to rectangles and continuous glass, in terms which might have given increasing consideration to the demands of human comfort and the sense of locality—a more subjective simplicity for every purpose; not merely the plainness that results from exploring the dead-end path of elimination.

Early European theory without doubt had identified functional methods with glazed, cubic forms. The world had accepted this identification and had contrasted the cube with various traditional or sentimental images, including the cosy cottage, which represented non-functional methods. Design-for-use was a sort of moral anchor stabilizing the twentieth-century movement until the mid-century mark. Then, gradually, the more intellectual and sensual delights began to beckon creative architects again. The frankly non-functional nature of the Farnsworth and Johnson glass houses indicated some impatience with the anchor. Mies van der Rohe adopted the discipline of technology. Philip Johnson gradually drew away from all external disciplines, relying on his own scholarship and taste to protect him as he returned to the enjoyment of irrelevant beautiful form. Cautiously, tentatively at first, over the next few years in the early 1950s more elements were introduced in flagrant defiance of Functionalist ethics.

One of the first moves was to revive the arch. For fifty years no self-respecting twentieth-century architect would have dreamed of making the top of a door or a window anything but straight and flat, as dictated by the steel or precast concrete lintels which spanned them. It was true that the arched shape had a certain amount of logical justification in brickwork and concrete. Would it be a denial of the old moral anchor to leave out the steel or concrete lintel over an opening in a brick wall and to span it with a pretty arch of bricks? Many architects comforted themselves with a negative answer as they thus began the long drift away from the straight and narrow path laid out by the pioneers. Round arches were followed by parabolic and pointed arches, and arches of more exotic curves. The roof line was subjected to the same examination. After fifty years of flatness it humped up again into gables and hips and vaults of many strange contortions. At the foot of the United Nations' glass gravestone to Functionalism Wallace Harrison built the conference building with a fashionable, meaningless draped curve broken by a central dome. All of this and much more was done by serious architects working within the limitations of the traditional structural systems and familiar materials. Sometimes with the engineer's help they went further. Not infrequently they shattered all the moral rules that had been established painfully since the middle of the nineteenth century. It was sad for the older men who had participated in the fight for a rational architecture to see this delinquency growing. One could sympathize with the younger men's feeling of boredom towards the box, but not with the loosening of the morals. There was no need for it. The anchor had become repressive, blocking a healthy desire for more visual excitement. Yet there was no need to cut loose from it in order to explore architecture further for more visual stimulation.

Notwithstanding the confusion at this time, there were then as always some accepted architectural standards. It was possible in the early 1950s (as it is still possible now) to imagine a building that commanded universal admiration. The Parthenon was one; and the pyramids. Most of the cathedrals lengthened the list. Regent's Park Terrace, the Bath Circus, and others of Georgian England could be added without argument. Some colonial adaptations of these in America and Australia could receive the same sort of unanimous approval, and could carry the list into the nineteenth century, if no further. The reason for the universal approval of certain buildings through the ages could be explained readily enough. All of them possessed a quality in sufficient strength to determine architectural merit and override such considerations as whether, in the historian's eye, the style happened to be describable as International Style or Georgian or Gothic. All buildings of universal admiration had

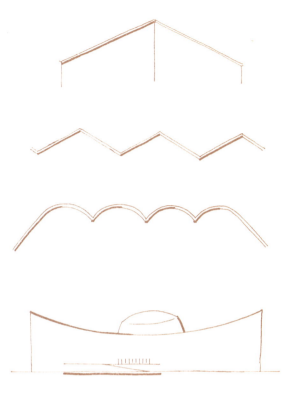

some seemingly original and clearly valid idea permeating every part of them, unifying them with nameless character.

When present in other arts this quality is generally recognized and acknowledged, and no one seems to find it necessary to attempt to name and define it. The work may be fitted into some style category, but it will be permitted its individuality of character. In the appreciation of architecture, however, style and character tend to get confused. Architectural critics were more inclined than those of the other arts in the first half of the century to think in rigid terms of style. They loved to type each guide-solution. In the matter-of-fact way of the drafting office they liked to see character tied down to a sort of contract specification and all buildings neatly fitted into labelled pigeon-holes. The architectural world in the 1950s at least was still tied to style, at home with style, and fidgetty when confronted with character.

Yet the fact was that the ethics and techniques of Functionalism were capable of being developed into a wide range of characters, and only one narrow range of expression had been attempted by the pioneers. The adopted character could be described as light, clean, fresh, open and simple, and these were the words used with dulling monotony to describe a thousand glassy cubes of the early 1950s. Light and clean had become the almost universal emotional expression, a deadly constant of architecture. Perhaps the most humilating slight to the status of the mother art during this period was the common use of the word 'beautiful' as highest praise. 'Beautiful' was used solemnly in the sense of 'pretty', meaning no more than unoffending tidiness. Self-respecting arts had banished the word in this sense before the turn into the twentieth century. Architecture's passive acceptance of the implications of such an indeterminate term of praise put her in the intellectual company of the interior decoration magazines or Hollywood, where an approved pattern of artistic behaviour was established, where aesthetic right and wrong were defined, and achievement was measured in the ability to work in the established idiom in such a way as to lull the observer to sleep.

Architecture had come to accept a sophisticated but essentially chocolate-box ideal of beauty, or prettiness; a timorous, sedate desire for conformity of the form and spirit of every

76

building. The twentieth-century movement which had set out with crusading zeal to purge building of false styles and free it for the expression of reality had declined to a flat state. In the hands of masters like Mies van der Rohe and Philip Johnson the glass cubes could still be exercises for intellectual or artistic refinement, but in less subtle hands they had lost all meaning outside technology.

Thus the *avant-garde* or architecture, the third generation of the twentieth-century, came to tire of the movement at the middle point of its career. Young architects revolted against the light, simple, clean, uncluttered look of their teachers' work. The serious-minded rebels argued that the old morals were too re-stricting. A world built of clean, uncluttered forms would carry architecture into a decline to unplumbed depths of ennui. The less serious-minded revelled in the cutting of the moral or Functionalist anchor, and delighted in the return to arches, roofs, and historical allusions.

The twentieth-century process which began with the elimination of ornament, and pressed on rapidly to the elimination of visually complicated details of construction, had passed to the stage at which creative young men felt that the elimination of architecture itself was in sight. So they turned their backs on the goal that once seemed so desirable. They insisted no longer on a physical justification for everything. Many pronounced openly, or in so many words, that the world had passed the stage of Functional-ism.

At this pronouncement there was an almost audible sigh of relief from the salesmen of industrial bulding materials. The decade after the World War II had produced a great increase of synthetic and composite materials from the chemical laboratories: materials that lent themselves to numerous enticing and meaning-less shapes and effects. The choice of surface materials, of grained, gilded, grilled products, had been embarrassing. It was still indigestible, but now the moral anchor was cut the embar-rassment was gone. Prominent and respected architects began to use such frivolous materials and to suggest further develop-ments for them. Then the period revivals began. It was sad indeed for the old men. It was the end of the revolution.

Part Three | COUNTER-REVOLUTION

At the outset the counter-revolution against the International Style was not led by some young upstart who had never known or responded to the lessons of the first phase. On the contrary it began most unexpectedly as an inside job, a coup by a defector from the old school, none other than Edward Durrell Stone. Stone had been one of the leading pioneers of the International Style in the United States and was the architect, in 1939, of the symbolic, glassy, cubic box for the headquarters of the Museum of Modern Art in New York. Now he launched an attack on one of the most cherished beliefs by beginning a new search for sophisticated richness in surface treatment.

Edward Stone had helped substantially to promote the perfection of the glass box and the American public's acceptance of it, but he did not taste popular fame until he began to dress his disciplined plans in fancy materials. In 1955 he began to stimulate the unresponsive public eye with a romantic chiaroscurist splendour quite unfamiliar after two decades of shadowless boxes. His stylistic swing was gentle and took him through several gradual steps. His first move was the U.S. Embassy at New Delhi.

This was classically square and disciplined in plan but was dressed up in frankly Taj Mahal atmospherics. A grille of perforated blocks in interlocking square-and-circle pattern wrapped its foursquare plan. Gilt, shimmering metal and water were added with the sure hand of a tasteful Cecil B. De Mille. Then came a pill factory in Pasadena, which, with rather less reason to be Eastern, had even more pools and many more grilles. Both these buildings, despite their romanticism and surface frills, were members of the modern movement. They were the International Style gift-wrapped. But the very presence of the contrived decorative effects, however sophisticated, broke the spell of the modern pioneers' fundamental law that every element must be useful and even more important—as in justice—must be seen to be useful.

Once started down the by-road from New Delhi, there seemed to be a fatal fascination to reach the end as soon as possible. The ornamentation was not in itself the chief affront to the principles of the old twentieth-century architecture. It represented a general drift away from the realities of the function to literary associations and symbolism, to prettiness or beauty for its own sake. The new tightly self-contained forms, as in the precise

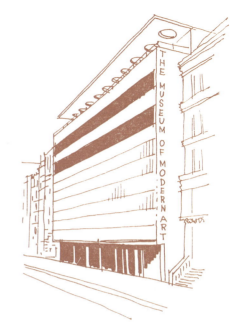

The Museum of Modern Art

U.S. Embassy at New Delhi

81

square doughnut at New Delhi, was a decisive return to classical symmetry and a final affront to the functional articulation of the Bauhaus vision.

For the kind of ornamentation adopted at this time by Edward D. Stone and one or two of the members of a younger generation of American architects, including the brilliant Japanese-American Minoru Yamasaki, was essentially different from the ordinary kind of ornament that had never left the vulgar market even at the height of the International Style's influence.

The decade of the 1950s might have been one of skirmish and confusion in architectural circles, but in the sumptuous world of interior decorators, home magazines, and manufacturers of surface treatments the sky had never been less clouded. Their ornaments were indirectly influenced by the architects' activities during the first phase of modern. They were inclined to be more cubic and glassy, lighter and cleaner and more uncluttered. Plain bold colours and geometrical patterns of stripes, checks and spots replaced flowers and fruit. Yet the old gentle, savage urge to decorate every useful object had never been seriously touched by the architects' moralizing. In their honorary task of making all they touched bright and gay and a treat to the wandering eye, the leaders of popular visual culture could now call on a wider range of materials, pigments and textures than ever before, but their principles were still much the same as when they used fretwork and gargoyles. False effects, as of marble in plastic floor tiles and timber grains in laminated sheets and golden metallic surfaces on cardboard, now enlivened their cheerless carnival world. Their object was, as ever, to keep the eye entertained, the vision filled to capacity with as many features and contrasts of shape and colour as possible. A home was made more diverting when the brickwork was relieved by contrasting panels of feature bricks or veneer stonework, if the bathroom were custom-decorated in two-tone tilework or paint in alternating primary colours, if the pastel paints on the plaster walls were contrasted with a feature wall of grass paper and the hard industrial lines of the kitchen equipment were softened by fine etched lines like lingerie.

Thus by the process of division the Featurists made their Contemporary carnival. And thus they continue today in restless confusion, and will continue so long as integrity and meaning in the design of useful objects have no claim to public respect. The artistic unity of any building, such as, for example, a house, is first divided by the Featurists into a number of individually conceived, unrelated spaces: for instance, feminine master-bedroom in pink frills, masculine boy's-room in knotty-pine, neuter living-room in limed ash. Then each space is splintered into a number of separate visual effects: a rugged stone fireplace contrasted with gleaming metal trim contrasted with flounces of candy-striped fabric. The have-nots of taste love lots of separate things, and when presented with a single thing must break it up into odd pieces. At all costs they want to avoid the boring mono-tony of artistic unity. They want as many elements as the eye can take in: colours, textures, ornamental surfaces; all more than half-consciously symbolic of good living and worldly success.

The social and economic influences at work under the Featurist skin may be obvious enough, but the artistic origins are more oblique. The restless richness in popular Contemporary design is the International Style gone wrong. Sad to say, it is the illogical conclusion on the popular plane of that sober, austere, puri-tanical movement. The Featurist Contemporary decorators developed or perverted the pioneers' idea of articulation, the Bauhausian separation and expression of elements, without of course accepting the discipline of the architectural theory that went with it. They destroyed the Gropius scale. They went further than any of the pioneers intended in the celebration of unrelated pieces and the destruction of wholes.

This popular seduction of the intellectual idea of articulation seemed to sully it in the eyes of sensitive architects and they turned away from it as they had turned away from the anti-ornament ethics. The various movements into which twentieth-century architecture split at this time may have seemed very different on the surface, but had in fact a strong initial impulse in common. It was the one glimpsed in Philip Johnson's glass house: a new search for artistic wholeness or unity in each design, for monolithic form, for the monumentality which had been conspicuously missing from architecture since the new movement began.

The essential idea of twentieth-century design, total functional simplicity, was not new in 1900. In a sense it was older than the Acropolis. All that was new in 1900 was the strict, literal, unbending interpretation of the idea. In a similar way in the 1950s the one consistent idea which seemed to be taking shape in the mists of architectural thought was no new idea, but a new attitude to another old idea. It was an unbending, literal interpretation of the classical concept of total unification by design.

Total is the important word, just as *total* simplicity was the key to the first revolution of modern architecture. Serious architects have always worked to a theme of sorts and have always believed their buildings to be reasonably simple. Even the most frenzied of Victorian decorators liked to think of their works as irreducable. The degree of simplicity and unity is what matters. The early modern architects went back to the utilitarian tradition of barns and bridges in their absolute ban on ornamental effects. Now some fifty years later an equally drastic and fundamental revision began overtaking the popular form of architecture. Starting some time about 1955 every new building of self-importance sought to be a single thing. It was no longer content just to be composed, integrated, co-ordinated by a regular module, a balanced assemblage of parts. It was not content even to look like an organic growth. Suddenly every important building wanted to be a self-contained, finite, closed form—to be based on a monumental and monolithic idea.

It would be impossible to put a precise date on the beginning of this monolithic movement. Perhaps its first spectacular manifestation was Eero Saarinen's Kresge dome at the Massachusetts Institute of Technology in 1953, a closed form based on a monolithic concept if ever there was one, and in strong contrast to the wandering, if controlled, compositions of Saarinen's earlier successes. But Johnson's glass house might be considered the prototype. Long before either of these, Frank Lloyd Wright had published his designs for the most monolithic of all his works, the Guggenheim Museum; and years before that, in 1932, Buckminster Fuller produced his early designs for a 'Dymaxion' industrialized house, a hexagonal container hung on a central mast. In fact one can quite easily trace isolated origins back through Erich Mendelsohn's sketches of plastic one-piece structures to the beginnings of twentieth-century design. But in

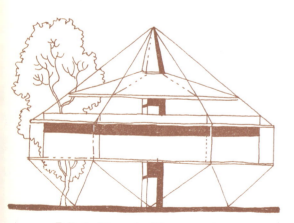

Fuller's 'Dymaxion' house project

the later years of the 1950 decade the monolithic idea became a passion, or a fashion, and many of the apparently unrelated stunning experiments of the leading architects of this time were, in fact, only different means adopted by different men to create the same desired oneness of visual effect.

The puzzle which these men set themselves was to find one form, one single idea, that fitted each practical planning problem set to them. This form, when found, was bound to be uncompromising, and the observer's eye was inclined to accept or reject it immediately without need for contemplation. The object of a monolithic design was to organize all the functions to be sheltered, and all the materials suitable for use, into a single mass. Architects who were not impressed by the monolithic tendencies of the time argued that it was morally impossible to discipline functions and materials so severely without in some way distorting them—in short, a monolithic solution was seldom an honest solution. Yet despite this suspicion, most architects could readily understand and sympathize with what the monolithic school was attempting to do, for in a less rigid way, in a friendlier spirit of compromise, a monolithic vision is what any serious architect always has hoped for every time he has sought a guide solution or visual goal to lead him through the maze of puzzles set by his client's building problems.

Nevertheless, in forcing such solutions against the natural flow of functions, the monolithic movement seemed to be looking back a long way behind the birth of twentieth-century architecture and the theories of articulation and functional expression. They harked back to classical design concepts, back to a Platonic aim of perfection of form. The monolithic movement was certainly not interested in expressing function. It was not necessarily keen on expressing structure, although it was interconnected with some vigorous new structural exploits which we shall examine presently. It was not always interested in expressing anything or in what was expressed, but only in the essential rule of form which made expression possible.

As new form-explorers soon rediscovered, there are three main, basically different kinds of guide visions which assist in the making of a monumental, monolithic effect. The most common and only strictly correct vision is a box, or case. One selects a

Mendelsohn's vision of a factory

A restaurant by Richard Aeck

Concrete house by Johansen

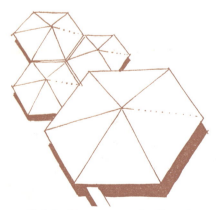

Matched luggage, or family style

likely-looking single container of finite, closed form and fits into it all the necessary parts of the building, like packing a suitcase. As it happens, the most common box is usually about the proportions of a business-like suitcase: it is the international modern glass-box office block. Another monolithic guide vision may be based on one of the devices used by Frank Lloyd Wright to achieve Organic growth patterns; to make the structure one-piece but cellular, like a honeycomb, or a bunch of grapes. One selects a likely-looking unit of space for the building—say, the bedroom-bathroom unit in a motel, or the classroom in a school—or a structural element such as a mushroom column and one makes the whole building a multiple of similar units or cells of space, with no distractions. This technique usually turns out to be more practical than the most flexible of suitcases, because the grape units may be placed anywhere that function dictates, and the overall shape of the building may sprawl anywhere that the occupiers desire, without the unity being destroyed. For a bunch of grapes is still a single thing no matter how ungeometrically and disorderly it grows.

Each of these two principal means of achieving a tight, intense unity in the building has many possible variations, and a number was seen at this time. The suitcase could be purpose-shaped in the way of a violin case, hinting at the things it contained. Conversely it could dissolve into quite a loose, flexible thing like a plastic shopping-bag full of mixed fruit, as John Johansen demonstrated in his suggestion for a house of free-formed shell concrete in an amorphous but continuous, and still single, shape. Sometimes the container took on proudly exotic shapes, symbolic or evocative of some aspect of the building's purpose, as in a number of restaurants and churches of the period. Sometimes when one suitcase was found to be inadequate to hold all the required elements of the building the architect resorted to the use of a few extra, smaller containers, making each of these a miniature of the dominating one, matching in shape and materials. He thus achieved the unity of a porter's trolleyful of matched luggage, or a family of mother duck and ducklings. But whatever strange shape the container was given, or whatever combined form—matched luggage, a family, a bunch of grapes—the significant thing was that the noun was singular in the *avant-garde* about 1960: the essence of each design solution was the combining or merging of several things into one thing.

Sometimes the individual grape in a grape-bunch solution was an exotic fruit, as in the purely decorative and frivolous United States pavilion at the World Agricultural Fair in New Delhi in 1960. Minoru Yamasaki, its architect, made a golden Eastern dome of thin moulded plastic the design-unit, or grape. He repeated this many times high above the pavement and could have added as many more domes as suited the whim of the exhibition authorities without embarrassment to the unity of the bunch. The grape unit was less exotic and more functional in the United States Consulate at Tabriz, Iran. It was not at all decorative but convincingly strong and structural in the folded concrete units of Paul Rudolph's Sarasota High School. Again, the grape became a practical solution to the industrialization of house-building in some standardized prefabricated space-units proposed by George Nelson and Gordon Chadwick.

There were of course other variations of the two main techniques. Twins appeared. A few years earlier if an architect had found it necessary to build two similar buildings—say, two apartment blocks—beside each other, he would have gone out of his way to avoid what was considered one of the worst design *faux pas*: duality. Probably he would have made one of the buildings tall and thin, the other short and fat; he would have composed them as two things, leading your eye gently from the squat to the tall one. But in the sixty-storey apartment blocks in Marina City, in Chicago, designed in the late fifties, Bertrand Goldberg made a giant building two things, but identical: tall thin cylindrical monoliths, so that they were in effect one thing: twins, a pair. Later, in 1963, Minoru Yamasaki designed the world's highest building, New York's World Trade Centre, on a similar concept, except that his twin monolithic towers were square. The original guide vision among modern twins was perhaps the Mies van der Rohe apartments of 1956 on Lake Shore Drive, Chicago. But then in a sense the whole monolithic movement was begun by Mies, for it was made ethically tenable by his reversal of the slogan of early modern architecture: 'form follows function'. The architect's duty in the technological age, as he demonstrated it, was to build perfect structural form. The function would fit in. He

New Delhi pavilion by Yamasaki

U.S. Consulate at Tabriz by E. L. Barnes

World Trade Centre by Yamasaki

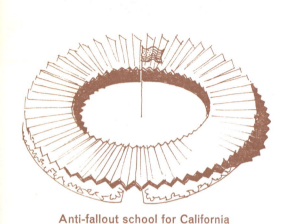

Anti-fallout school for California

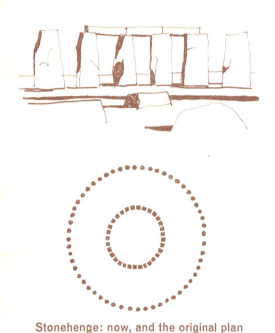

Stonehenge: now, and the original plan

spent his creative life perfecting the technology and character of the glass suitcase as non-emotional abstract poetry. Meanwhile his reversal of the old Functionalist principle had set others off, freed of ethical inhibitions, on a delightful search for beautiful form. In seemingly no time many architects in many parts of the world came back from the search triumphantly carrying the one shape that Mies van der Rohe himself would never use (unless, as he said, they began making steel in curves): a circle.

It was not just coincidence, and not simply fashion, but by 1960 the circle was almost as common a guide vision in creative architecture as the rectangle had been a few years earlier. The circle was translated into the three dimensions of a usable building in a dozen ways. It became a cylinder, or a dome, or—most frequently—a ring, as in a fairly classic and symbolic example: the anti-fallout school designed by the Californian Institute of Architects' Committee on Nuclear Energy.

The emergence of the circle from the rectilinear background of modern architecture was not surprising, since monolithism was a deliberate movement away from the intellectual, functional/structural rationalizations of the early modern towards a scholarly, neo-classic approach.

Another similar but more prudent move was to compress the ubiquitous rectangle into the tighter geometrical shape of the square. Hence the number of office tower buildings of this period which were exactly square in plan, like Yamasaki's Michigan Consolidated Gas Building in Detroit. But a circle was far better; more classical, closed and complete.

The circle is the most self-contained, precise, concise shape, recurring at intervals throughout history in the plan of special public buildings from Stonehenge on. Turned into three-dimensional form, as in a dome, the circle suggests the arch of the heavens, the sphere, the divine form of a drop of water, or the earth, or the universe.

The mystical connotations here are not irrelevant. Partial responsibility for the revival of circles must be accepted by Professor Rudolf Wittkower, whose learned treatise on the mystical influence during the Renaissance of Pythagorean and Vitruvian theories of form, *Architectural Principles in the Age of Humanism*, was required reading in most architectural

88

schools in the period after World War II. The ancients saw cosmic significance in involved mathematical analogies between music, geometry and the human body. They would have delighted in the form of hundreds of new variations on the circle and the dome which now appeared every day; for instance, Roy Grounds's design for the Academy of Science dome at Canberra, 1957, the Borodino panorama building in Moscow, or a dozen projects for dome-homes, or the two complimentary buildings for Brasilia's Houses of Parliament by Oscar Niemeyer: one a plain conventional upright dome, the other a matching upside-down dome, or bowl.

Borodino panorama building in Moscow

Mystiques apart, the circle and the dome were economically justifiable. They are nature's way of enclosing the greatest volume within the least surface. Working from the other side without a trace of mysticism and strictly within rational engineering principles, the Italian engineer, Pier Luigi Nervi, frequently produced a circular plan and a domed form for his intricate ventures in concrete, seen at their best in the stadia for the Rome Olympic Games of 1960.

The sudden interest in monolithic effects reflected a new attitude to the matter of scale, which affects all architectural visions. If, for instance, an architect of the early high Functionalist era designed a model community, he would articulate separately the commercial, industrial, cultural, religious and domestic areas and give all these separate architectural expressions on his drawing-board; but he would probably be content to leave each separate house as a simple block. However, when asked to detail a house, he would articulate and express as separate boxes the living, sleeping, service areas and the garden shed. Finally when he concentrated on the shed he would articulate and express separately the places for the hand-tools and the heavier equipment and would probably provide a circular place for rolling the hose. This illustration is intended to suggest that articulation was essentially not a practical or functional scheme but an artistic idea which could be expanded or contracted in interpretation to suit the will or whim of the designing architect.

In a similar way, but in reverse, scale affected the artistic idea of monolithism. Even in the Functionalist days an architect

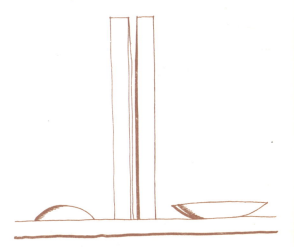

Niemeyer's Government Centre in Brasilia

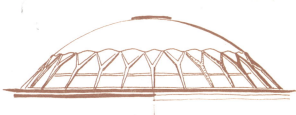

Nervi's Olympic Games stadium in Rome

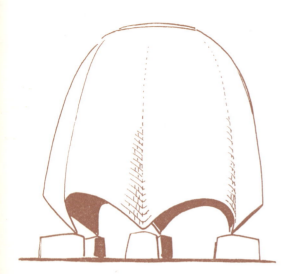

Shrine at the 'roofless church' by Johnson

La Tourette monastery by Le Corbusier

might have imagined a monolithic concept for a building with a function as simple as that of a small shrine—although few would have turned the suitcase into such an exotic bag as Philip Johnson made for the so-called roofless church at New Harmony, Indiana. As the movement developed, and designers kept tightening up their architectural themes, it was seen that more and more complex functions could be packed into bigger and bigger suitcases. The circular vision stretched to take in a whole jet airport in Kansas City, a whole college community for six thousand students in Raleigh, North Carolina, and a whole city in the Horizon City project in Texas by the Brazilian planner, Lucia Costa. When asked to carry the more complicated functions, however, even the biggest suitcases or grape-bunches had their practical limitations, illustrated in the ragged edges of the Horizon City scheme. Only in a dictatorship or a classical Utopia would you expect everybody to conform uncomplainingly to some allotted compartment in a cosmic dream. Without doubt many architects of this period were searching for something cosmic or elemental, certainly far removed from the mundane rationalism of the International Style. Consider La Tourette, a Dominican monastery in France by the greatest of the rationalist pioneers, Le Corbusier. At first glance this had the faint suggestion of a suitcase, like most of Le Corbusier's works, in the overall rectilinear form. But it was certainly not a case you would be proud to claim in the baggage room; it seemed to have been deliberately broken into bits. For Le Corbusier was not attempting to make a single thing in the direct visual sense; but in a poetic, harmonic and rather excitedly mystical way he was harking back to ancient dogmas of proportion and rhythm.

The whole of La Tourette was designed on the 'Modulor' scale, Le Corbusier's own measuring device which was in itself a thorough-going renunciation of the kind of solid rationalist logic of the International Style to which he was a parent. The Modulor scale was based on the ancient mathematical proportion known as the Golden Section or Golden Cut (a line divided so that the smaller to the larger part is in the same proportion as the larger to the whole): a rule which would have had no meaning at all to the early heroes of the modern movement. Moreover, the whole of the three-storey window wall of La Tourette which looked down a long valley was designed in the visual equivalent of the proportions of a musical composition. Le Corbusier sought the collaboration of a musician-engineer colleague, named Xenas, for this task. He called the activity 'Metastasis', which is a name for a chemical transformation. No doubt Le Corbusier saw the wall thus transformed from a number of pieces of timber and sheets of glass into a single harmony. In this he demonstrated the third method discovered so far for achieving a monolithic effect. This method relates more to technique than to conception. It consists of relating the pieces of one or more materials in so positive a manner as to swamp visually all other materials and even the form of the building. The Japanese are masters of this method.

In all other monolithic design, form is paramount, and thus the central stage of design, the conceptual step, is all important. The architect spends much time in his scrabbling and sorting of the puzzle pieces, and in his contemplation of them he searches for something beyond the physical matter of the pieces. He looks for more than an acceptable suitcase to carry them. He seeks the vision of an ideal suitcase, one which suggests by its shape that it is ideally and uniquely appropriate for the carrying of the functional requirements of the problem in hand. It is not necessary for an architect to have access to pencil and paper for him to achieve a truly monolithic concept. It is so simple and inescapable that he can see it in his mind and hold it there intact as long as necessary. Proportions, scale, balance, are irrelevant. Every exciting suitcase conception since the Tower of Babel has this visionary quality.

In a pure case of second-phase modern architecture the exact solution to the building problem is discovered, not by any kind of engineer or social scientist, not even by a clever designer— but by an inspired dreamer, instantaneously, in a flash when the clouds part and all beauty is revealed to him. That is the nature of a grand monolithic concept; or, should we say, that is the desired effect. And a vision is characteristically a single complete thing, not a lot of things beautifully composed, nor a single thing intellectually analysed. The architectural translation of such a vision also will have the power of instantaneous communication, and if the message received in a flash does indeed appear to be highly appropriate for the human problem of shelter under consideration, then it can be judged that the suitcase is likely to be good architecture. The problem of the visionary architect, however, is not to seek visions, which are easy enough to cultivate, but to train himself to dismiss irrelevant visions.

'The search for significant form', as it was sometimes called, continued to capture many architects' attention through the 1960s, and will always be likely to do so, for the indisputable, definable object of all design is co-ordination: the drawing together of many parts into an apparent wholeness, a singleness of purpose. It is only right and proper and historically correct that a building should have a recognizable idea running all through, and it is exciting and stimulating when the idea is so vivid that it makes an immediate, imperative image. But the key questions in judgment remain: is the strong, vital image the right one for the task in hand? Is it functionally and structurally reasonable? Or is the architect falsifying some functions to make the form so succinct and complete? Is he merely recalling some previously successful shape with nostalgia but no relevance?

These questions disturbed the Functionalists of the old school even when the monolithic forms were plain, as they were, for instance, in Saarinen's work. Yet sometimes they were alarmingly ornate. Edward Stone went several steps further than the New Delhi Embassy when he built the Huntington Hartford Museum, completed in 1964, at Columbus Circle, New York. It had a Venetian arcade ornamented by verd-antique marble medallions; it was an exquisite chocolate box rather than a suitcase.

Edward D. Stone's adventures in ornament impressed a number of architects, and many who, unlike him, had never been really at home in the twentieth century, were relieved to see the pioneers' firm discipline broken by one of the old hands. Grilles of various sorts appeared all over the world. A perforated concrete block was made in Australia with the trade name 'Edstone'. In many architectural offices decoration was again considered respectable. But not in all.

Most thoughtful or ordinary architects were not yet ready to dismiss so lightly the accumulated principles of a century of attacks against applied ornament. Stone's supporters might

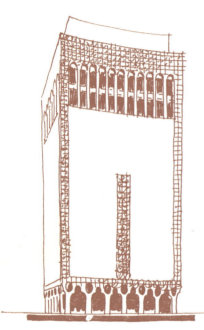

Huntington Hartford Museum

argue that his work retained and even improved upon the essential simple imagery of the modern movement, but to most architects simplicity still meant more than lack of clutter. It meant the indivisible quality of 'nakedness', as Greenough saw it in 1852, 'the majesty of the essential instead of the trappings of pretention'. Perhaps Adolf Loos went too far in his famous essay. Perhaps ornament was not exactly akin to crime, savagery, depraved sexuality; but many would still accept his thesis that the 'evolution of human culture implies the disappearance of ornament from the object of use'.

Thus Stone's example was unacceptable to many who were equally bored by the plain white boxes. They turned instead to search for new visual interest in the shapes of the structure itself. Those who turned to the exact square were able to play with all the ordinary criss-cross structural methods. Those who adopted the various circular forms in most cases could adapt conventional structure without difficulty and with some radial enjoyment. But the biggest strides were taken between 1953 and 1955 by a number of respected architects who made radical assaults on all traditional geometrical forms. One of these was Le Corbusier, and his assault, made in 1955 before La Tourette, was so powerful and so contrary that it threw the whole world of architecture off balance. Le Corbusier, for all his Modulor mysticism and the romantic language of his writings, was regarded as a solid pillar —one of the original *pilotis*, indeed—of the glassy cubist International Style. He had sometimes played with free shapes on the periphery of his buildings, but nowhere in his work or writings had he prepared his great world following for the thing he built at the top of a hill at Ronchamp in the south of France. It was Notre Dame du Haut, a chapel for pilgrims, and it was built practically without right-angles. Although its main interior space was in overall shape conventional enough to take rows of pews with an altar at one end and a chapel at the side, no regularity was discernible from the outside, for the walls twisted off-vertical and the roof swept out far beyond the walls in a great brown-coloured upturned brim like a tricorn hat. It was as if Le Corbusier had deliberately set out to smash every rule of twentieth-century architecture that he had once helped to build up. The interior space was not of much consequence whereas the white external

Notre Dame du Haut at Ronchamp

93

form set against dark hills and seen by pilgrims from miles away was conceived as a sculptural monument, a modern Parthenon. The concrete was hugely oversized for the tasks it was given: the walls were visibly several feet thick. All regularity was lost in a random scatter of tiny windows filled with coloured glass as ornamental in its own way as Gothic tracery. Nothing could have looked less machine-made than this building; on the contrary it seemed to have been pushed about by hand while still wet. Indeed Le Corbusier demonstrated his old-fashioned craftsmanly sort of love for it by not being able to keep his hands off it. He did paintings on the doors and he scribbled things in the glass panels. This was perhaps the final gesture of renunciation of the original twentieth-century credo, for Adolf Loos had had some rather strong things to say about the infantile urge to scribble on walls.

Ronchamp was a bombshell. Not only was it iconoclastic, coming from the hands of a master so closely identified with Functionalist theory; it also came at a time when confusion already strained morale in the ranks. It was just too radical, too far away from the comprehensible central stream, for words. So most of the words that did come from the critics were inclined to be evasive. Ronchamp was written off as a whim of a master who had stayed on the straight and narrow track long enough to be permitted a single digression or aberration. One could hardly deny that it was a moving experience to stand in the open air court before the chapel when pilgrims arrived or to feel the soft interior curves respond to their prayers. But in a way this was an irrelevant building; in architecture's stream it could be explained away as overgrown sculpture by an architect who clearly thought of himself as a Leonardo-of-all-trades. It was not necessary, most critics decided, to reconcile the Ronchamp curves with the straight lines of established modern architecture, for it might not happen again.

Of course it did. In the next few years curves as unorthodox as those of Ronchamp were to become common. Certainly curves had been seen before in the twentieth century. Several of the most famous Functionalist buildings featured prominently semi-circular elements in their plans: for instance, Gropius's Werkbund exhibition hall of 1914 with its two famous bubble staircases, and Le Corbusier's Villa Savoye of 1929 with its semi-cylindrical wall

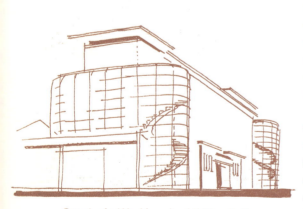

Gropius's Werkbund exhibition hall

94

on the ground floor guiding and expressing the flow of traffic around the carport. Even irregular shapes had honoured precedents. In Le Corbusier's famous Swiss Pavilion at the University of Paris the ground floor annexe and one wall of the multi-storey slab were bent arbitrarily. But up to this time, no matter how freely any walls might wander or curve, the final enclosing element—the roof—was essentially box-like: a flat lid.

In *Space, Time and Architecture*, the canonical document of the first phase of the modern movement, Dr Giedion called attention to the unexplored possibilities for imaginative design, within the Functionalist code, above head height—above the reach of function, as it were. He referred to the 'unsolved vaulting problem of our period'. He pointed out that in the Baroque period architectural vision pressed to the very end of constructional recourses, whereas in this century 'there are available to us constructional possibilities which we have not been able to exploit to anything like their full extent'. What the modern movement needed, he wrote, was 'architects who know how to stir the imagination of the engineer'. In response, the *avant-garde* looked up to the roof. Overhead, out of reach of the practical hands of time-and-motion experts, they found indeed exciting promise of an honourable escape from the functional discipline.

In short, an important swing that happened during the war-time pause in building was a transference of attention from walls to roof, or rather to a combined wall-roof. Although the architects might not have realized it at the time, the significance of this change of emphasis was that it made necessary a *rapprochement* between the master designers: the architect and the engineer. Earlier twentieth-century essays in plastic form were tentative enough to be muddled through practically without consultants. Mendelsohn's plasticity was as superficial as a thick sauce poured over conventional structure. Even the wanton walls of the Swiss Pavilion were roofed by a thick flat slab, the design of which would not baffle the most modest architectural office. Yet the idea of plastic structure in a roof curving threateningly overhead demanded much more than schoolboy mathematics and, about 1950, sent the architect back to the engineer, humble if not yet completely cap-in-hand.

The engineer's response was good. As a matter of fact, while

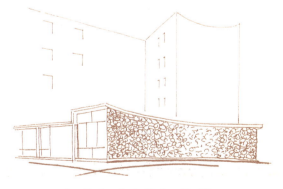

Le Corbusier's Swiss Pavilion

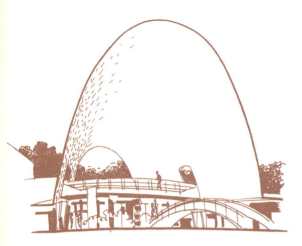

Maillart's Cement Hall

Candela's shell for San Antonio

he was away working on his own he had developed, after some sad failures, a proficiency in two important new branches of structure. One of these was shell concrete, which had hardly been used in building apart from a simple parabolic vault of concrete in Maillart's Cement Hall in the Swiss National Exhibition at Zurich in 1939. Its unexplored prospects seemed enormous, especially when one thought of possible applications to building of the fascinating shapes of advanced solid geometry. The engineer could indeed assist the architect, and throughout the 1950s an extraordinary stream of strangely-shaped buildings flowed from the collaboration. At no time did this stream grow wide or deep enough to affect ordinary professional or commercial building, but for some years it dominated the architectural journals, the undergraduate studios, and architectural discussion. It seemed to indicate clearly a major change in direction of twentieth-century architecture.

Some of the new shapes were as free and arbitrary as those of Ronchamp, but these were rare and atypical. The quality which bound most of the new shape buildings into a new movement was that they possessed the structural inspiration and justification that Ronchamp lacked, although some of them no doubt had as well more commercial justification than their authors were prepared to admit. All of them were moved by the same mood of rejection of the right-angle that affected Le Corbusier. These buildings with warps, waves, folds, droops and other unexpected shapes stood out sharply against the square glazed grid walls of the first phase, which by this time had been popularly accepted at last as modern architecture. They were reminiscent of the kinds of sweeping curves seen on graphs, on stress diagrams glimpsed over an engineer's shoulder, and usually they demonstrated in clear sign language some structural principle that was new to building, though often known well enough to engineers.

An engineer, not an architect, was in fact the new hero: Felix Candela of Mexico. Candela's concrete vaults, exploiting the strength of a curved shell, like an egg, were made for churches which others fitted out. They performed exciting structural gymnastics in subtle geometrical shapes. His most photographed work, which symbolized or summarized the new movement, was the church San Antonio de Las Huertas designed in 1954, and built by 1959. Its extraordinary shape was indescribable in conventional architectural terms. Its combination walls-roof vaulting was like a billow of canvas, a tent out of control on a stormy night that was snap frozen and later, after the wind dropped, found standing on the four pointed corners that formerly tethered it to the ground.

These vaults were in fact saddle shapes, and this was the most exciting of all new shapes that assaulted architectural conventions in the fifties. The saddle is a plane twisted, or curved in opposing directions. Imagine a simple saddle of plastic material: a square laid diagonally on the back of a horse with the two corners in front and back of the rider turned up and the other two turned down to hug the horse. It happens that a doubly-curved plane of this shape can be made up entirely from straight lines and is then a pure geometrical form called the hyperbolic paraboloid. The fact that such fascinating curves could be constructed of straight lines—straight lengths of building timber or steel—justified them on economic grounds, and, almost, on the old moral grounds. In any event, who cared about the old morals any more? Other hyperboloids appeared. Concrete-shell engineers examined every possibility. Le Corbusier made the Philips Pavilion at the Brussels World Fair of 1958 by combining a number of extremely sharply twisted metal hyperbolic paraboloids. Candela produced an extraordinary atmospheric interior with as many twists, curves and points as any Gothic cathedral in the Virgen Milagrosa church near Mexico City. He also showed in a couple of factory buildings that the warped plane could be repeated and repeated in orderly rhythm over a big space with as much economic and functional justification as an asbestos-cement saw-tooth roof.

Waved or serpentine walls and roofs of the kind introduced in serious buildings early in the fifties were everywhere exploited commercially by the end of the fifties, for they lent themselves to shop verandahs, restaurant canopies and other semi-functional, semi-advertising applications. The strength of a thin-folded plane, familiar in a paper fan, produced walls and roofs zigzagging playfully, or bouncing along in a series of vaults. By easy degrees it began to dawn on architects everywhere that a reasonably functional box need not necessarily be rectilinear everywhere

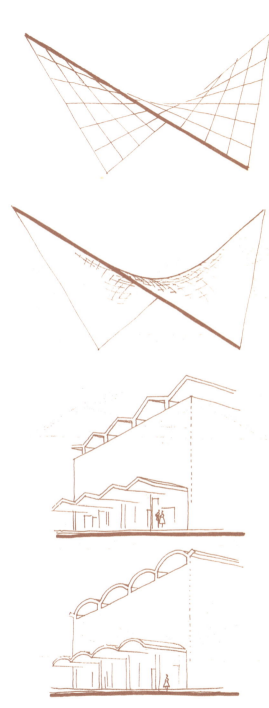

and they pestered the engineer for more exciting and reasonably rational ideas for enclosing space.

All these unfamiliar curvings and twistings, and this new reliance on free engineering exploits, were not without precedent in the story of modern architecture. For years the twentieth-century movement was proud to look back to the middle of the previous century and claim antecedents in London's Crystal Palace and Paris's Galeries des Machines and Eiffel Tower. Those great exposition structures were designed by engineers but were still classifiable as architecture, and they had the feel of machinery and industry which quickened the twentieth-century pulse. The new exciting engineering recalled those great curving structures of a century ago. But they were also dangerously reminiscent of something much less reputable and closer to home. Such unexpected twists, curves and zigzags had been decorated camp followers of the modern movement for a quarter of a century. The Jazz Style, the Ultra-Moderne, the Modernistic, and lately the popular Contemporary, had all used a sort of mad professor's geometry to catch the passing eye. In Britain designers called this disreputable design 'Borax'; in America it was sometimes called 'Googie', after a remarkable Californian chain of restaurants that liked to look as if they had been through an earthquake. The Googie stylists made shapes for the sake of shocking. The new exciting engineering had no such base motive. Everyone in the know could easily distinguish between the two types— although, unfortunately, the number in the know included few enough people outside the professions of architecture and engineering.

The new architecture of the new shapes cut new ground. It was unrelated to both precedents. It was not simply providing new solutions to old structural-functional problems and it was certainly not done merely commercially or frivolously. It may have marked the beginning of the warmer collaboration between architecture and engineering which developed through the 1960s, but it was not in the same class as the equally extraordinary shapes of unselfconscious engineering, as found in unquestionably practical machines, bridges, scaffolds, and so on. In the new-shape architecture the vehicle may have been structural but the initial thrust came from outside the engineer's office.

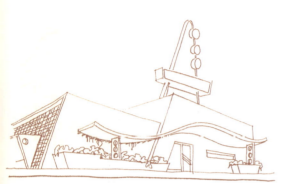

Googie shape of the forties

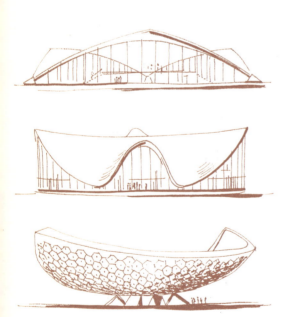

New shapes of the fifties

98

The shapes in themselves were not essentially new. The principles of the zigzag fold and shell concrete had been understood many years before. They were not more functional or economical than a cube. Indeed some of the new shapes demanded elaborate methods—such as, in an extreme case, a formwork laboriously built up of compacted earth for a multicurved concrete shell—which contradicted the technological and social developments of the twentieth century. The new search for more interesting shapes would have been philosophically possible at any time after the birth of modern architecture. Indeed, if Erich Mendelsohn had had the clients with enough money and Antonio Gaudi of Barcelona had had contact with the right engineers, both of these might have produced similar shapes a generation earlier.

The new-shape search had various motives not directly connected with engineering but directly connected with the post-war psychology of the 1950s, for it was at this time becoming clear that the first generation of modern architects had handed down to the new generation something much more important than the glass box. The glass box was only a symbol of an idea that they had: an idea of creative realism in the face of the new conditions that had struck the world with the Industrial Revolution. Now after two world wars a new twentieth-century generation faced a new set of conditions. It needed to find something new in architecture, partly just for the sake of newness, not because of any disrespect for the old masters; on the contrary, out of respect for the worldwide aesthetic spring-cleaning that was their greatest achievement. The new generation wanted to be as brave and as inventive as the pioneers of the century. It was not questioning the box and the curtain wall. It accepted and respected them. Yet as the public resistance to the box melted away, as the International Style grew respectable and commercial, many architects of more inventive or explorative nature began to feel a great impatience to see what lay beyond the curtain. Some undoubtedly had grown tired of the twentieth-century revolution and wanted to tear up the code that had led to the box. Others still believed in the code but felt that they would be respecting it best by trying to find new avenues for it beyond the curtain wall.

Many men drawn to the practice of architecture have a little in

Barcelona apartment house by Gaudi

99

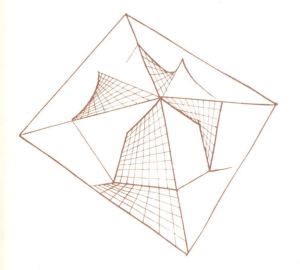

them of the gadgeteer and the inventor. Many are encouraged by the ambivalent nature of their calling to think of themselves as little Leonardos, and of architecture as a catalyst that can and should merge the incompatible natures of art and science—a bridge between the two cultures as suggested by C. P. Snow. The modern fragmented world of specialists, however, is impatient with any man who thinks he has many parts. It selects the parts it likes best and may give him credit for these, but anything else he wishes to do in another field is inclined to detract from rather than add to his prestige. This attitude seems infuriatingly stuffy to men with octopus talents and they try earnestly to excel in the opposite direction just for the sake of confounding the dullard specialists. Thus Le Corbusier has wanted always to be acclaimed as a painter, and Frank Lloyd Wright wanted to be recognized as a master engineer. And the ordinary architect of the fifties, who usually by nature, training and tradition believed himself to be equally proficient in art and science, wanted greatly to gain more recognition for what his left hand could do in the latter field than for what his right was doing in art. In this new nuclear age he was often rather embarrassed still to be considered just an artist. He would rather invent a new structure than contrive a new spatial experience.

An engineer's perfectly balanced form and an artistic vision of monolithic form were marvellously complementary. They combined to consolidate the counter-revolution. Architecture suddenly had no time for loose or expansible themes. The shapes most proudly prized were closed and finite. Hence the resounding success of the hyperbolic paraboloid and its numerous groupings in tight mathematical bunches as demonstrated by Eduardo Catelano in 1956. Then as an extension of this concept another partial reaction set in against another tenet of the pioneers. There was a perceptible swing of the pendulum against the idea of universality in modern architectural theory and a hankering after the particular, the exclusive, unique poetic expression for each occasion.

However much the great men of early twentieth-century architecture resented the term 'International Style', it could not be denied that their methods became international and universal. Moreover there was an attraction in the idea of universality. Each new building seemed to assert that its solution to the given problem was the only right one, the final word on the subject, and should be good enough without further investigation for all future buildings of the same kind. Each building was expected thus to exemplify some pure and perfect theory capable of universal application. Perhaps minor adaptations within the theory might be necessary to suit regional or climatic differences, but this would not invalidate the universality of the idea. The International Style had no time for theories that were not as wide as the world.

Monolithic concepts, whether of a conventional kind or of new and exciting structure, violated this tenet. Architects who remained loyal to the old Functionalist school shuddered when faced with most buildings of the counter-revolution or second phase of modern architecture, not only because they were often less logical functionally or structurally, but also because they were conspicuously once-only creations. So at first the structural-shape buildings met with an unenthusiastic reception. While they could be, and frequently were, called exciting by non-critical observers, others were neither excited nor amused. The Italian engineer, Pier Luigi Nervi, condemned Saarinen's three-cornered dome at the Massachusetts Institute of Technology as an illogical shape, abusing structural laws, and he added in general censure: 'Today structural ideas are invaded by extravagance and they are deprived of all justification.' The critic, Sybil Moholy-Nagy, retorted at another time: 'Who would be so rude as to demand a view of the *exterior* of a Nervi hall?' Many less renowned critics and numerous ordinary architects showed plain bewilderment at the suddenness of the counter-revolution against the plain modern architecture for which, only a moment ago, everyone of progressive good-will had seemed to be crusading.

The new curved forms seemed to point around a corner in architectural development. Certainly they were visually stimulating; but were they valid, rational, genuine? How could they and the glass box both be right? Pity the poor, ordinary bothered practitioner! At this time he was quite lost. Surveying the Massachusetts Institute of Technology dome and his mixed-up colleagues of the post-war decade, the Italian architect, Eugenio Montuori, said, 'The mess is complete.'

The shape-race developed more rapidly than any of the other styles of the fifties. The contributory elements converged into a movement in a matter of months about 1954. During this time Ronchamp and the Massachusetts Institute of Technology dome were completed and Matthew Nowicki's great saddle-shaped State Fair Arena was built, after his death, at Raleigh, North Carolina. The little town of Raleigh was in fact a nursery of the non-rectilinear rage, for no shape building was more convincing or influential than Nowicki's arena, and nearby in a suburban street Eduardo Catelano built for himself a timber warped-roof house which had almost equal impact on the domestic level. By late 1956 the rage for structural shape had littered the draughting rooms of every architectural school in the western world with cut-outs of twisted and folded cardboard, wire, rubber and matchsticks. Several prominent buildings on the crest of the first wave soon became famous and created world reputation for their young architects. These included the St Louis airport by Yamasaki, and the Sydney Opera House by Joern Utzon. Yet this was by no means a young man's rebellion. Several of the old guard who had nurtured the box were in it too. Apart from Le Corbusier's Ronchamp, there was at least a suggestion of the new shapes in Gropius's design for the University of Bagdad, and in the UNESCO building in Paris in 1957 Gropius's old colleague and Bauhausman Marcel Breuer, with others, produced a conference room annexe with a wide span roof folded like a concertina. Admittedly this structure was atypical in its lack of curves. However, it did possess the essential quality of the new guide vision: its main walls and its roof were conceived as one.

In some of the exciting-shape buildings the excitement was confined to a roof resting on a structure and plan of conventional bearing. These were only tentative or transitional members of the movement. Their roofs were separate elements and as such could not be considered as much more worthy than any applied decoration or other publicity device. If they constituted the entire movement, it would deserve no more attention than any transient decorative fashion. But they were not all, and some of the irregular buildings demanded most careful consideration. These were the many buildings in which the theme shape made up virtually the entire building. The plan, the traffic flow and all the functional

Breuer's conference room for UNESCO

accents related to the curves and the odd angles of the structure. Foreign elements were negligible. Usually these were confined to the thin framing members of the glazed sections of the exterior, which were always an embarrassment in exciting concrete structures. Some brilliant single-minded shapes of this sort were conceived, and the better they were the more they showed up a fundamental anomaly in all curved buildings, plain or fancy, indeed in all buildings of unorthodox shape, angular or curved. For the modern age gave architects much freedom with one hand but took some away with the other.

The advanced engineering techniques which made possible such exciting shapes, such flights of fancy and daring architectural expression, on the other hand insisted continually on more conformity by the architect to the standardized machine-made ingredients. The more energetic the structural gymnastics, the more obvious the conflict was likely to be, for only the structure was freed. In the 1950s more and more of the accessories were becoming almost as essential as the structure: lifts, lavatories, air-conditioning equipment, glazing members, and so on, not to mention sandwich panels and window frames and metal doors and a hundred or so pieces of packaged mechanical equipment. All these things normally were mass-produced, and mass-production involuntarily dictates an anonymous, conventional, usually literally square sort of shape. In nearly all the exciting buildings there were awkward corners and secret pockets where flowing shapes conflicted with rectangular services.

Eero Saarinen said at this time, as he toyed with the fluid shapes of a new building: 'Architecture is only worth doing if you can make all one thing of a building so that every detail dovetails with every other detail and supports the whole.' Yet there can never be any real dovetailing between sculpturally curved concrete and the shaft of a mass-produced elevator. One way to achieve the desired dovetailing would be to discard all the advantages and economics developed over the years in the mass-production of building elements and to have the equipment custom-built for each building in sympathetic curves. The only other way would be to encourage many more buildings to have the same sort of curves that have been selected for your own solution, and to persuade the manufacturers to mass-produce all the necessary

103

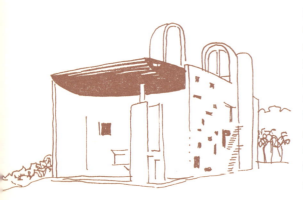

The rear of Ronchamp chapel

equipment in curves at the same prices as their normal rectilinear merchandise. But this would remove the justification for the sculptural and structural gymnastics—that they produce the unique, poetical architectural quality in answer to a specific problem. The more that an irregular building approaches the condition of being 'a whole thing', the less it is able to take advantage of being made in the twentieth century. It is restricted from dipping freely into the larder of mass-produced equipment. Le Corbusier was able to keep the Ronchamp shape almost a whole thing because it was not serving a twentieth-century function. It had no equipment, and one straight wooden staircase at the back was the only reference to twentieth-century democratic functions such as fire-escapes. Le Corbusier decided to be frank about this, and the stair shatters the fluid harmony of the rest.

The buildings which followed the exciting shape guide vision were in fact highly significant because, of all the new styles of the fifties, they were least expressive of mass-production techniques, and were indeed anti-universal, reminding architects that all the technical potentialities of the twentieth century were not bound to mass-production. The structure was still free, more free than ever before, and the architect still had every justification—indeed a duty—to exploit this freedom whenever the opportunity arose, by creating forms and spaces precisely appropriate to the occasion.

Of course it need hardly be stressed again that the new shape style was by no means the only serious architecture of the fifties. All the time the glass box continued to prosper. The style that Mies van der Rohe had developed out of the Bauhaus method was still the basic and most widely accepted modern guide vision. Firms like Skidmore, Owings and Merrill in the U.S.A. had made something fine, creative, and commercial out of it. The box was the popularly accepted office language of the fifties, complete with its own limited vocabulary. Mies van der Rohe was the one old master of the century not to be caught up in some degree by the new mood. 'I don't want to be interesting,' he said in 1956, 'I want to be good.' He trusted that his designs threw out everything that was not reasonable. He pointed resolutely to a future of universal, impersonal envelopes. He had minimum difficulties with recalcitrant lift shafts. Sometimes he could find in the trade catalogues no suitable mail chutes, fire alarms or other fittings for his proudest buildings, and he would insist on redesigning them, or designing special ones. This was not as precious as it might seem. He redesigned not to make ordinary industrial products special for his building, but to make them less special, less noticeable, more universal, anonymous and characterless, to de-style the industrial design.

Yet there were several things in the Mies code that were interminably criticized by many observers. As everyone knows, the general public as a whole loathed the lack of privacy in his noble, exposed, vulnerable spaces. Professional critics looked closer into the glass and queried the reasonableness of some of his more technical architectural preoccupations. For instance, the redundant steel uprights applied to certain concrete columns to complete the rhythm of window mullions on his Lake Shore Drive skyscrapers in Chicago. His great respect for arbitrary laws of proportion seemed to be 'interesting' rather than objectively reasonable and 'good'. Reasonableness is always relative to the accepted code. The great value of Mies as a leader was not that his followers' work was more reasonable but that it usually succeeded in being, as he wished, less 'interesting'. It was impersonal, taciturn, expressionless—all qualities which the first generation of the twentieth century could respect as being clean, unsentimental and honest.

A world designed by Mies van der Rohe and his followers was and still is an acceptable idea to anyone whose taste has not been entirely jaded by the appalling everyday architectural background. It would be uninteresting enough to offend nobody. It might not be interesting enough to please many, but that is preferable to the other extreme. A world in which every building was an exciting shape designed by a Candela or a Saarinen at the high pitches of their respective imaginations would surely be acceptable to very few people. It would be a maniacally interesting prospect. But, happily enough, a choice between the two will not be given to architecture. The second prospect is impossible. The examples of high acrobatics and high poetry will always be isolated incidents, simply because of the inherent nature of the acrobat and the poet always to be in a minority, no matter how

Lake Shore Drive apartments

high are raised the levels of the common physique and the common prose.

The glass box and the anonymous curtain wall could make a suitable universal backdrop to life. They accept commercial exploitation with more dignity than any other style since commercialization of architecture began. Acres of glass walls such as occur nowadays in the financial district of any big city form an acceptably plain, impersonal, workaday background comparable to the eighteenth century's repetitive urban facades. Such a background would be suitable for silhouetting a foreground of special gems of the sort for which the 1950s was tirelessly seeking in monolithism and shape-engineering. At least this concept of a duplex architecture, of background and foreground, was a reasonable compromise in a theoretical attempt to restore order to architectural thinking in the divided and confused fifties. At no time, however, did it appear to be a practical proposition. Too few owners and architects would be prepared to take their place in the anonymous background; most would be diverted against their consciences by the commercial need to advertise or the egotistical urge to raise monuments to their own inadequate ability.

The danger of a fascinating mathematical shape like the hyperbolic paraboloid is that it is neither fish nor fowl, neither the jewel nor the black velvet. It is neither uninteresting nor flexible enough to be extended as an acceptable universal background and it does not promise all that could be desired in a foreground gem. The single saddle shape was used in its pure form in the middle fifties for a farming pavilion, a political hall, a few houses, a restaurant or two, and in countless other modest workaday projects from motels to churches. The power of its compelling shape was soon dissipated by this indiscriminate use. It offered an easy, all too easy, formula to the advertiser and the egotist—a prefabricated emotional stress like a stock suspense situation in melodrama. Nevertheless, the structural-shape movement kept galloping ahead to new fields. One of the most promising and revolutionary was that which was opened up in 1952 by Matthew Nowicki in his Raleigh pavilion: tensile construction.

The principle of using the strength of materials in tension, as in a hammock, rather than in compression, as in a feather bed,

106

was not new. Tensile or tension construction are names loosely given to any system of building that relies more than usually on the enormously increased resistance of some materials, notably steel, when stretched rather than compressed. For instance, it is clear that a long thin column of steel will bend under any substantial load and collapse, but the same steel bar reversed in the structure so that the load hangs from it, stretching it, will carry tons. In this way a thin steel bar can do the same work as a thick column of brick, stone or mass concrete.

The history of tension construction goes back behind the grass rope spans across Tibetan gorges to some of the earliest human shelters slung between trees. Even in terms of modern engineering, tension and suspension were old in 1952. Steel suspension bridges were some of the proudest and most spectacular exhibits which the engineering profession produced at intervals over the century following the successful pioneering of the principle in Thomas Telford's Menai Strait Bridge of 1826. Tension was not even a new principle in everyday building construction. For centuries it was well understood that the most conventional structures harboured tensile stresses, and that their strength could be greatly boosted by introducing metal at points so affected, preferably when no one was looking. The mighty domes of St Peter's in Rome and St Paul's in London would collapse but for the series of chains that bind them around their bases and hold them from spreading. Many less renowned old buildings are held together by iron tension rods bolted through their cracked walls to S-plates on the outside.

Nearly every conventional structure, of course, has some members that act at least some of the time in tension, just as every one of the new buildings which were now called tension structures had some compressive members. What distinguished the latter type was not simply a higher proportion of tensile members, nor an architectural emphasis on these. The key was flexibility. A structure seemed to qualify for the tension title if its main members were by nature limp, worthless in compression, and relied on tension to hold them rigid enough for the job in hand. Cables, rods and thin steel flats were its usual media. Even on these terms, tension was a full century old. For the New York World's Fair of 1853 James Bogardus proposed a hanging

French pavilion at Zagreb

roof of sheet iron suspended as a saucer no less than twelve hundred feet in diameter. The idea of making suspended flexible cables an architectural theme was pioneered between the wars by Simon Breines and Josef van der Kar in their entry for the Palace of the Soviets competition in 1932, and by Bernard La Faille in a French pavilion built at Zagreb in Yugoslavia in 1935. The latter gave a bold demonstration of the simplest kind of suspended roof. It was a cylindrical building covered by a shallow saucer of sheet steel resting on a single cartwheel of cables—the form probably used by the Romans for the velarium that sunshaded the Colosseum. Its curve was the curve of a chain hanging free between two points and known as a 'catenary'. This was a word overworked in drafting rooms in the late fifties.

The Zagreb pavilion was a building of considerable temerity. It was apparently protected by its comparatively modest diameter of 110 feet, for it innocently ignored the problem which later preoccupied suspension design. Fifteen years after it was built, when architects began to examine cables again as a means of climbing out of the box, the innocence was gone. The image of serene, suspended catenary curves was haunted now by a nightmare vision of Tacoma Narrows Bridge. This was the most elegantly long and slender bridge ever built, a graceful half-mile of hanging roadway at Puget Sound. Four months after it was opened in 1940 a newsreel camera was at hand to photograph it fluttering in a medium wind, oscillating, twisting and finally racking itself to bits. The ugly tangle that was left in the water afterwards was a terrible lesson to a generation of engineers not to underestimate the phenomenon of flutter.

The problem in building roofs was to find something more positive than the simple action of gravity to counter the upward pull of the suspension cables. This led to the idea of introducing more cables with a counter-downward-pull, thus developing a dynamic equilibrium irrespective of gravity. This might be marked as the subtle point of change between suspension and tension structure.

After the brilliant pioneering proposals as early as 1926 by Buckminster Fuller, the first tensile structure to break into the architectural press was Matthew Nowicki's livestock pavilion, and it deserved its fame. It was totally and eloquently a tensile structure, as single-minded as a student's project in cane and rubber bands. What was more, it worked. Its saddle of prestressed counter-acting cables weathered two major hurricanes shortly after completion, and laid the spectre of Tacoma. Fred Severud, who supervised the pavilion after Nowicki's death, went on immediately to less fashionable success with a weighty concrete composite saddle over a cafeteria at the Corning Glass Works, designed by Harrison and Abramovitz. The engineer, Frei Otto, who visited Severud during the Raleigh project, went home to Germany to build, and encourage the building of, several tension roof structures, and to celebrate the arrival of the new structural system in *Das Hangende Dach* (The Hung Roof), published in 1954. Otto stressed the problem of anchoring tension structures, explaining that the economies gained in the lightness of the span may be lost on the buttressing required to hold the ends, and he suggested tying the ends of tension cables to existing natural or artificial buttresses: for instance, roofing a valley by anchoring cables in the surrounding hills.

Yet, as often happens, the roving eye of the progressive architect was not caught by these worthy attempts to conquer the structural and economic complexities so much as by one or two quite modest structures which ignored most of the engineering problems, but caught the spirit of tension with style and formed the basis of a new guide vision. One of these was Powell and Moya's 'Skylon' of 1951, the theme structure for the 1952 Festival of Britain, a 'dangerous toy', as it was called, with a cigar-shaped pylon suspended above ground, demonstrating effectively the aptitude of tension for acrobatic balancing feats. Another about the same time was even smaller: Twitchell and Rudolph's tiny house of about 800 square feet on the edge of a Florida bayou, a glass box shaded by louvres and covered by a catenary bow that shot Paul Rudolph, in his early thirties, into the front rank of the rising generation of post-war architects. The span of the catenary was so small—less than 22 feet—and the effects of wind buffet and suction consequently so slight, that the structure could get away without stabilizing devices. The steel flats supporting the roof deck hung simply, almost limply, between wooden posts which were guyed back by steel rods to the ends of protruding floor beams. The beams, rods, threads, plates and nuts were

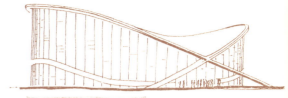

Livestock pavilion by Nowicki

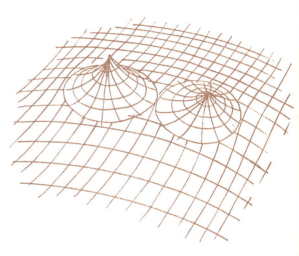

A hung roof proposed by Otto

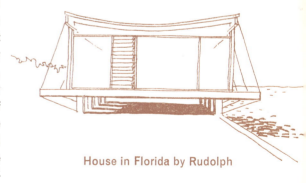

House in Florida by Rudolph

all openly displayed. Because of the diminutive scale the structure had no engineering excitement. Moreover it did not carry resounding conviction from the logical or practical points of view, for there are easier ways to span 22 feet. The success of this nice little cabin was won entirely on architectural grounds. It was an early demonstration of the essence of tension structure in visual terms. It threw some light on a neglected branch of architectural aesthetics, in which complementary values to those of conventional compression structures might apply.

Every traditional ethnic division of architectural beauty before 1920 was based on some sort of empathy with earthbound solidarity and stability. The modern movement rebelled for a time against such stodgy, reposeful design, and played with propping buildings high on posts, called 'pilotis', and on balancing massive loads on cantilevers. The attraction of those structural devices to artistic rebels of the early twentieth century was that they enabled mass to have practically no visible means of support. They borrowed the excitement of the magician's art of levitation, and the effect usually was a statement of defiance of the classical rules. But the architectural quality of tension structure was clearly different again. The means of support were likely to be as apparent in their own distinctive way as a row of classical columns. Tension was not the way of the magician, but of the trapeze artist, on the breathtaking high wires under the big top.

The importance of a clear and honest expression of structure was one of the main tenets of twentieth-century architecture. Pier Luigi Nervi was one who always believed that clarity and beauty are one. In simplified engineering language he explained, 'the intuition and sensitivity to statics, which in a more or less confused form may be found in all people, are satisfied by those structures which immediately reveal the play of forces and resistance'. Unfortunately some admirable compressive structural systems are inherently secretive. Both sides of a concrete shell, for instance, can never be seen at the same time. Thus even the eye of the *cognoscente* has no means of judging how elegantly thin or clumsily thick the shell is and must rely on prior information or the unreliable evidence of the edges. But in tension structures, at least, the play of forces and resistance are instantly revealed under normal circumstances. Unless the structure is shamefully clothed, tension is inclined to explain itself in a most articulate way. The tensile member communicates its task and some impression of its load with clarity to the dullest child familiar with the behaviour of string or wire in his toys. Such thin members cannot conceivably be pushing; unquestionably they are pulling or being pulled. The way such thin pieces drape themselves, or droop under weight, or bend suddenly at point loads, or if freed spring straight to the shortest cut between two points which want to separate—this behaviour makes up the language of tension and the spirit of the tensile guide vision.

In the early 1950s tension rivalled shell concrete as the chosen medium of the *avant-garde*. Students laboured over projects in matchsticks and cotton. Progressive designers strung almost anything from the ceiling: bookshelves, tables, shop counters. Three separate continuous catenary systems were used for a house near Melbourne by Kevin Borland with engineer Bill Irwin in 1952. They were made by draping reinforcing mesh over convenient supports and spreading a thin layer of concrete on top. With spans of modest scale and methods of guying back at the ends literally down to earth, the tension structure proved to be a manageable and remarkably economical challenger to any of the cheapest conventional cottage constructions.

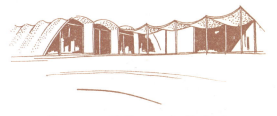

House near Melbourne by Borland

By this time it was apparent that two rather different practical applications of tension were emerging. One was two-dimensional, as used most directly in the Rudolph house. In this the tension system acted only in a series of vertical planes or portal frames. Usually each of these was formed by a catenary slung between two props which on the outside were guyed back diagonally to some kind of ground anchor. These portal frames were then connected laterally by conventional rigid ties. This system promised immediate economical, utilitarian results within the capacity of ordinary building practice and applicable to ordinary buildings, multi-roomed and rectilinear. In the second application, as seen in the Raleigh pavilion, the tension system was three-dimensional, finding equilibrium between counteracting pulls from all directions. Usually the tension members were flexible cables and the cradle to which they were anchored took a fine exciting shape in solid geometry. This system promised to be the more glamorous sister, applicable mainly to the enclosure

111

of big public spaces whose functional shape was more or less indeterminate.

In 1956 in Melbourne Bill Irwin was engaged on a major structure of each kind. In the first category, he completed an Olympic swimming stadium with architects Borland, Peter McIntyre, and John and Phyllis Murphy, and with the architects Yuncken Freeman he began the three-dimensional Sidney Myer Music Bowl. The pool building was exemplary two-dimensional tension design. The compressive props were sloped at about 45 degrees and were the principal functional members of the concept, for they also carried the spectator seating, facing the central pools. The back guys dropped vertically. The roof between the props was not made of flexible cables, for too much vibration would have carried through to the seating. Instead the wide space was spanned at each structural bay with a light diamond-shaped truss, which was stiff enough to resist objectionable vibration. Tightening of the vertical guys post-tensioned the horizontal trusses.

The music bowl shelter was an equally good example of three-dimensional tension. It lay within a fold of parkland that offered ground anchorage on three sides to a tension roof whose purpose was to shelter an orchestra stage and a few thousand people in favoured seats. Only two compression members were required. They finished as cigar-shaped props to hold a mouth open on one side to a larger audience on the lawn behind those seated. The cables were strung in counteracting tension, as at Raleigh. The main, longitudinal members swept up from the ground at the rear of the stage to a massive cable strung over the props and forming a lip to the mouth. Lateral cables were pulled over the top and tied down each side.

The shape was not precisely predetermined. Cable lengths were adjusted to mould the form to the architect's taste and the engineer's two guiding rules: to maintain a double curve at all points and something close to a right angle at all cable crossings. Finally the upper cables were tightened, pulling down on the draped longitudinal cables and prestressing the system. The covering of aluminium-faced plywood panels was tailored to the cable grid. The heaviest live load that ever strikes the structure in practice puts the system, not into greater tension, but into compression, since the long, draped lower cables suffer an

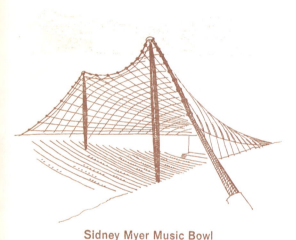

Sidney Myer Music Bowl

additional tensile load which is only a fraction of the relieving or compressive force enjoyed by the upper cables.

About 1957 both the freshly-proved kinds of tension structure had established themselves as guide visions and were applied in many buildings throughout the world. Two-dimensional systems were adopted by some airports for no reason but economy. At Kansas City, for instance, acres of column-free housing for aircraft were created by hanging corrugated concrete roofs of enormous size like wings from either side of an unimaginatively utilitarian workshop block. Also in 1957, Hugh Stubbins promoted the simple cross-cabled saddle to its first monumental task, in the Congress Hall of Berlin. Somehow it did not seem ideally cast for the role, and the inherent delicacy in the light roof was finally lost in concrete compromises with the massive structure below.

In 1959 another celebrated architect tried his hand with tension: Edward D. Stone built the U.S. Pavilion at the Brussels Fair. He introduced to one of his characteristic decorated monolithic conceptions a new and different attempt to rethink and perfect the earliest and simplest form of tension roof: the wheel over the pill box. In the past the wheel usually was simply a cartwheel made with flexible, radial cables. This soft cartwheel was draped, Dali-style, over open space. It trusted to gravity to hold it down and to luck to keep it from excessive vibration. About 1957 some rather crude if successful efforts were made to prestress or stiffen it. For instance the soft cartwheel over a circular stadium at Montevideo, designed and built by L. A. Mondino, L. I. Viera and A. S. Miller, was loaded with thousands of bricks during construction. While thus extended, the precast slabs that lay on the cables were cemented; then the bricks were removed. The main advance at Brussels was that stability came from a geometrical cable system capable of being prestressed—that is, made rigid by tightening. The 330-foot span of the pavilion was roofed with a double system of spokes, radiating from the top and bottom of a central cylindrical hub. It was a rigid, triangulated system, as in a bicycle wheel, which naturally was the name immediately given to this kind of roof. An incidental improvement was that the top of the roof was now conical instead of concave. Rainwater now drained to the outside wall where it could be disposed of simply. This eliminated the old embarrassment of having to convey the

U.S. Pavilion at Brussels

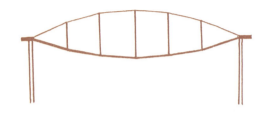

water that collected in the centre out to the perimeter by means of hanging pipes.

About the same time, engineer Lev Zetlin, working on the Municipal Auditorium for Utica in New York with architects Gehron and Seltzer, invented a subtle improvement. He tied two systems of unequally prestressed cables together by rigid vertical spreaders. The natural frequency of each set of cables being different, they were out of phase in any vibratory tendencies of one or the other. Zetlin, patenting the system, remarked that it could be suitable for spans of any distance between about 200 and 1800 feet.

Other new theories came to light in 1958. Led by Robert Le Ricolais at the University of Pennsylvania's school of architecture, students all over the world began exploring the field of tension and minimal surfaces, as demonstrated fascinatingly by the activities of soap films on twists of wire. Le Ricolais was not impressed by the wheel form, whether cart or bicycle, even over circular plans. He believed that triangular grid systems of cables without central tension rings were more promising.

Paul Chelazzi made one of the few proposals for the adaptation of tension principals to multi-storey building. He demonstrated a variation on an old device, which he called the 'Suspenarch'. This is a sort of coat-hanger for office floors. He proposed that it would sit on the top of the lift or service towers, erected first, and would drop tension cables to carry a stack of ten or so floors below. The 'Suspenarch' has a rigid top member bent in an arch and a cable connecting the ends, which sags the same distance as the arch rises. Arch and cable are connected at any suitable number of points along their length, and tension rods drop from the points of connection. The introduction of a light load-spreader like this, to substitute for a skyhook at the top of a building, improves the economical chances of tension in multi-storey work. Chelazzi became enthusiastic enough to envisage the idea developed in convenient stages up to a 300-storey tower, as innocent of architectural considerations as most visionary towers, including Frank Lloyd Wright's, have been innocent on the structural side.

Yet the man to leave all others behind in visionary projection of the tension idea was still Frei Otto. He pressed on from his studies of mechanically stressed membranes to the logical next step: pneumatically stressed membranes. His researches took two paths. One had been pioneered in Britain during World War I by F. W. Lanchester, who realized that the increase in normal air pressure required to hold a big balloon inflated was slight enough not to cause discomfort to an occupant. During World War II this idea was revived and in the 1950s balloon shelters served many practical purposes in a semi-experimental way. Blown-up plastic membranes were made as silos, sun-traps over pools, and shelters for conventional building operations in severe weather. The balloon shelter also had strong attraction for American travelling-exhibition designers, because it was the first structure since the teepee that could be rolled up and taken with you. In the U.S. Atomic Energy Exhibition which opened at Rio de Janeiro in November 1960, a balloon consciously became architecture for perhaps the first time. Like a great, obese, waisted white slug it sprawled on the grass, the clever prophetic creation of architect Victor Lundy, with construction by Walter Bird, assisted by Fred Severud.

U.S. Atomic Energy Exhibition hall

The other path of pneumatic structure pursued by Frei Otto was the way of the air-cushion. In this system the designer leaves the occupant normally pressurized but creates a rigid shelter over him by maintaining pressure between the double skins of a flexible covering. In its simplest, earliest form it was no more than a giant elevated circular air cushion, supported all round, a technical advance along the same lines as the first dished tensile roof. This kind was elegantly demonstrated in an outdoor theatre built in 1959 for the Boston Arts Centre, again by Walter Bird who by now was the Bird-Air Company, this time with architects Karl Koch and Margaret Ross, and engineer Paul Weidlinger. In more advanced applications the construction is divided up into some system of comparatively small and manageable pneumatic cushions.

Frei Otto took both these ideas and after much laboratory work with bewitching bubbles, cushions and balloons he published in August 1962 the first comprehensive report on pneumatic structures, *Zugbeanspruchte Konstruktionen* (Tensile Structures). Otto blew up the two pneumatic ideas seemingly close to bursting point, producing a breathtaking collection of schemes for super-

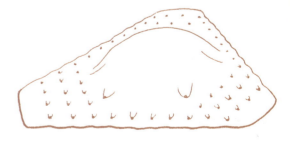

Pneumatic structure proposed by Otto

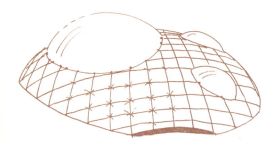

Allusive pneumatic structure

bubbles containing harbours, reservoirs, or cities. He also examined balloons. But the main interest in his profusely illustrated work still centred on the visual implications of pneumatic shapes, the bulbous curves that are familiar enough now in and around swimming pools, here expanded to vast proportions. In the course of his experiments he produced, with diverse practical demonstrations or applications in mind, multiple balloons with various strange effects. The most common was some fairly orderly geometrical variation on the buttoned cushion or rubber air-bed themes, but the more advanced suggested other images from modern life: perhaps an inner tube straining through a worn tyre, or a bulge of skin through a laddered stocking, or an eiderdown after a sleepless night. The associations were invariably non-architectural. Frei Otto's book heralded a medium of building that has no apparent reference to any style known previously outside science-fiction, nor to any canons of taste or judgment, nor to any recognizable aesthetic experience.

Thus architecture came to acknowledge tension as a major structural principle with unexplored applications and untold potentialities. It offers ample scope for visual inventiveness to maintain the interest of creative architects, and it holds out vague but tempting promises of economies to workaday builders. After 1958 nothing could hold back the steady growth of the tension vision and the tension principle wherever big spans were called for. A giant hangar at Idlewild Airport was built in 1959 at a cost claimed to be 60 per cent cheaper than a conventional structure. In the same year, the first wholly supported cable structure on the west coast of the U.S.A., a gymnasium at Central Washington College by architect Ralph H. Burkhard and engineers Anderson, Birkeland and Anderson, won a local American Institute of Architects Award of Merit. In 1964 Kenzo Tange completed the Tokyo Olympic stadia under the most imaginatively controlled multi-curved steel tents, shaped with a touch of Japanese tradition. In buildings such as these tension structure was visibly growing more assured. The Tacoma traumas were past. Tension began to communicate a sense of belonging in the workaday building industry.

Even now in the mid-sixties tension is very young and carrying a load of youthful problems. It is inclined to concentrate on rather

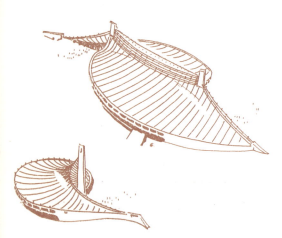

Tange's Olympic stadia in Tokyo

exhibitionist achievements and neglect its opportunities and duties in simpler fields such as housing. No significant development has followed its early successes in small buildings. Lacking co-ordinated research, its techniques are often quite crude: for example, the use of loads of bricks for prestressing even the smart-looking Villita Assembly Building in Texas. Then the novelty of some of the shapes is inclined to defeat them after a first successful showing. The most experienced architects, who should be coaxing the tension movement forward and helping to perfect its language, often will avoid using the striking shape again simply because it has been done before. Again, while schemes like Chelazzi's and Otto's send the mind racing ahead to all sorts of exciting possibilities, in practice tension is thwarted in many kinds of buildings by the requirements of fireproofing. Cables would fail in a fire, yet the bulk of the thinnest fire protection tends to cheat the method of its main advantages in spinning silk-thin webs. More basically, from the engineer's viewpoint the field of tension still has large uncharted areas. The behaviour of tensed materials is still by no means fully understood, even under laboratory conditions, not to mention the hazards of freak conditions in the field. The more enticing three-dimensional shapes usually cannot be analysed by conventional or any other known mathematical methods and the engineer sometimes must return to the spirit of the Middle Ages, feeling his way far out beyond the numbers. The architect, of course, is used to this sort of adventure, but nevertheless he would be happier to feel a confident engineer striding surely beside him in the dark. Yet even if the engineer were entirely confident in tension design the architect would still have plenty to do on his own account to reach understanding of the character of this reversal of familiar stresses.

The *rapprochement* between architect and engineer after World War II was welcomed immoderately by some idealists who believed that it heralded the end of the art-science split and the reappearance of a master-designer; architect and engineer rolled into one, to the great benefit of building. This worthy wishful thinking was hardly more logical than an argument that all other consultants—ventilating, acoustical, plumbing and so on—also should be rolled into the paragon. On the contrary, the extra complexities introduced by all the new structural methods were more likely to increase the number of separate building specialists. If the architect were to justify his own position as the top specialist, the specialist designer and controller, he had to keep alert. To be able to design successfully in any of the new techniques he had to be intimate with them. In the case of something as new and radical as tension he had to understand at least the laboratory behaviour, if only to know when to call the engineer. No less urgently he had to understand the visual qualities of tension character, which is a sort of negative version of compression character.

As already noted, the involuntary character of any correctly-designed tension member is not pushing, but obviously pulling. A major part of the conscious area of architectural design in tension must come from the visible degree of the pull as shown most clearly by the curves of the cables or membranes, especially when a curve changes in mid-length under a change of load. The first aesthetic rule of the genre is that structural tension need not be transmitted into emotional tension. Structural tension's mood, conveyed primarily by the visible pull of the members, ranges from the exceedingly highly-strung down to a relaxed droop. In the selection of tension for any job, the quality of the visible pull is worth at least as much consideration as the economics and the flutter.

In tension design the candid exposure of the structure is more than merely a moral or artistic nicety; it is practically obligatory to the peace of mind of those sheltered. While an exposed tensile member is likely to communicate its task with remarkable eloquence compared with most stolid compressive members, concealed tensile structure is likely to produce forms which seem alarmingly defiant of natural laws, at least to eyes accustomed to compressive behaviour. The need for some sort of false ceiling may do the damage, as in the case of the neat bandbox of the Villita Assembly Building, where an almost continuous ring of tidy acoustic panels slung under the drooping cables at a contrary angle gives a misleading suggestion of some insecure dome-like compressive structure.

For the same reason the frank exposure of tensile details is important to visual understanding. The joint between any two things in compression needs no explanation or celebration. The eye understands that the two things—suppose they are bricks— are being held together by gravity. Now it is often quite practical to treat joints between two things in tension with no more visual fuss than a joint between bricks. Perhaps they can be held together by a secret weld, or the joint may be hidden behind some sheathing. But the empathetic eye is undoubtedly made uneasy by such concealment. It knows the two things want to separate and is not really satisfied until it sees a firm grasp by one tensile member upon another, or upon something solid. Any direct and unselfconscious expression of this quality automatically produces the most eloquent explanation of the balance of forces. The effect is so different from anything known in compression structure that it promises the emergence, if treated well, of a new detail style, architecture's first prehensile style.

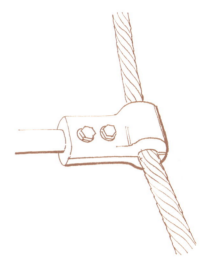

More fundamentally and much more importantly, the idea of tension seemed by the end of the fifties to be feeling its way to a formal expression, and this expression threatened the most cherished principles of form as known in this civilization. The predictable shapes of cabled membranes were an exciting novelty in the early fifties, but even the hyperbolic paraboloids were capable of conforming to known concepts of grace and beauty. Now in the sixties some of the shapes proposed in the more advanced reaches of the tension movement overturn practically all accepted values. Far more organic than the state ever approached by the most poetic compressive structure, the pressurized building is made in the image of a blood vessel, in man's image, though not, it must be admitted, in the image of the nicest looking man one has ever seen. Perhaps only because they are so young and inexperienced the balloons often tend to look so old and fat. An unemotional constructive approach to this kind of structure will frequently lead not to dullness but to a gross visual clumsiness which, seen through our conditioned eyes, can hardly be called anything but ugly. Yet in this kind of ugliness there may be one of the first really new keys to an escape from the historical vision that has been offered since the eradication of ornament. If that seems to be overstating the case, at least many architects of the 1960s could agree that the salvation of architecture from its danger of an accelerating backslide into irrelevant romanticism lay in the artistic understanding and development of all practical new ventures in building science. Tension promised a most revolutionary means of broadening the genuine expressive range of the medium. It promised a new language, virtually a new medium to architects, for use when the occasion permitted. It had its own qualities and limitations which called for mastery. Any architect using it correctly must finish with a form and expression radically different from the usual form of the same architect, however mature and settled in his ways he might be. Other structural and mechanical innovations as radical as tension may come to architecture from research laboratories as the century moves on. If welcomed in the right spirit all of them will extend greatly the expressive range of architecture without challenging any philosophical basis of design which happens to be ruling at the time.

Possibly the best way to put into perspective all the galloping developments after the mid-point of the century is to follow the activities of the undoubted star of the 1950 decade, the late Eero Saarinen, the great conceptualist, who first caught world notice in 1951 and enjoyed meteoric fame for just ten years until his death at the age of fifty-one. Among several great talents which Eero Saarinen possessed was the ability to sense a new movement or emotional change in the architectural climate just before it happened. Like a water diviner he was told by some mysterious means of an underground stream, and thus miraculously kept ahead of his eager generation and his restless decade. He was the first or equal first with all the styles of the fifties that we have been examining. Yet he discovered rather than made them. No doubt they would have happened in the same way without him. He was a compulsive explorer. Surely no other man who has enjoyed equal fame in any art has tried so many different styles in such a short time. He personified the architectural spirit of the fifties in his tensed, tireless, dedicated attack at the puzzle. At the end he was attracted to odd shapes, but like the 1950 decade itself he began quietly.

His career really started with the death of his famous father, Eliel, in 1950, and his first important work was done in the Mies image. The work was the supremely cubic, machinelike, regular, rectilinear and reasonable General Motors technical centre at Detroit in 1951. At intervals during the next ten years he would

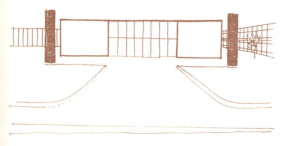

G.M. technical centre, Detroit

return to the Miesian rectangles: for instance, in the International Business Machines factory at Rochester, Minnesota, in 1956, and the Bell Laboratories in New Jersey—one of his last works, uncompleted at the time of his death. These were clearly appropriate occasions for the Mies approach, and he returned to it with an obvious surge of confidence. Between times he went as far out from this base as his imagination would let him, much further than any stretching of the early twentieth-century code would allow.

Saarinen himself said, 'There are many ways of being influenced by Mies. I would say that I have been most influenced by him in the Massachusetts Institute of Technology auditorium—not by his form, but by his principle of making the structure the dominant element in architecture and letting the functional ones fit in.' The M.I.T.—or Kresge—auditorium of 1955 was his first excursion into structural shape design. This tri-cornered dome-shape could be modelled by taking half a grapefruit on a plate and slicing off three equal segments until the remaining peel stood on the three points of an equilateral triangle. Indeed, according to a cover story on Saarinen in *Time* magazine a little later, this was precisely how Saarinen did devise the shape, at breakfast one morning, rushing the pared shell off to the office wrapped in a table-napkin.

The structural shell of the dome was, in his words, the dominant element, but it was not by any means a structural concept obedient to engineering principles. One fundamental quality of a domed structure is that its load is distributed evenly around the circle of the base. This quality was outraged by cramping the load into three tiny pointed shoes like the feet of a high-born Chinese lady. The dome suffered accordingly and revisions to the structure had to be made during construction. Again, it was not a functional idea. Saarinen managed to get the functional elements fitting in satisfactorily, finally getting the lid shut, but this success was not inevitable. This container was neither a soft-sided zipper bag, adjusting itself to what it accommodated, nor a violin case tailored to its contents. It was an inflexible piece of geometry: exactly one-eighth of a sphere, as it finished.

The open sliced sections were rather an embarrassment, as usually happens with voids in exciting-shape buildings. Regret-

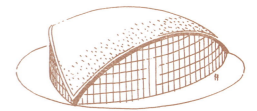

M.I.T. Kresge auditorium

121

tably they had to be filled in, to keep the rain out. A single sheet of glass would have filled each slice in a circumspect way, but technology had not and still has not risen to the task of making continuous glass sheets a hundred feet or so in length. Metal glazing bars are essential when making a big glass curtain, and these disturb the transparency and continuity. Nonetheless, Saarinen's curtain walls at the Massachusetts Institute of Technology were unobtrusive. But in order to make the building function internally only about two-thirds of the glass in the curtains could be transparent. A third of the glass panels had to be permanently opaque. Saarinen made them solid, but the colour of glass, a subtle grey-green which might have been a reflection of sky or cloud.

In short, the sliced dome was neither structural nor functional.

Then was it Expressionistic? Not really. It was in no way expressive of the musical concerts or meetings for which it was built. Again, it could have been made much prettier, much more visually satisfying, with more feet or with more projections above the bulging glass—if simple visual satisfaction had been Saarinen's aim.

The M.I.T. tri-corn dome was not a structural, functional expressive or visual idea. It was entirely an intellectual concept, as pure and cold as any International Style cube but suggesting a break free from the cube, a tentative side-step round the glass cube and the technological barrier.

Saarinen's next notable shape, designed in 1956 and completed in 1958, was the hockey rink at Yale. This began as a structural shape. The opposed curves of the saddle were enjoying wide academic publicity when he was planning the project. Eero Saarinen wanted to take the shape out of the field of the engineer's demonstrations and integrate it in a whole work of architecture. In effect he made a great tent of permanent materials, more relaxed than the M.I.T. dome and less pure in form. He shaped it, as he did many of his buildings at this time, against a mirror which represented the centre-line of whatever design eventuated. His modellers made to his instructions only half a model, while the mirror completed it. Any free movement and any sculptor's shapes made by Saarinen this side of the looking-glass were automatically turned into a symmetrical composition

Roof of the hockey rink at Yale

—that is, into architectural terms—by the reciprocal action in the reflection. He thus shaped to his satisfaction a piece of architectural sculpture that was an Expressionistic extension of an engineering concept.

He then pushed on beyond the engineering. He wanted to extend the two saddles which he and the mirror had formed on either side of the central humped spine. He drew them out longer, but at the same time he reversed the curves, turning the spine into the shape of a cupid's bow. This threw the tensile stresses of the cables in the saddle into confusion. It was an artistic or aesthetic concept flagrantly opposed to the mathematics.

In the tussle which resulted, Saarinen's enormous professional skill saw him through. Of course, the mathematics asserted themselves and gave him anguish at times, but in the long run he achieved a fairly convincing structural-functional form. The upright arch of the cupid's bow spine was matched by a reclining arch in a beam which ran round the back of the raised seating on each side. Thus the basis of the two matched saddles was framed, not quite arbitrarily, but from functional requirements. He managed to retain the lightness of the cable web, and almost made the tensile members and the compressive arches fall into an architectural whole. Only three stabilizing guy wires strung to the top of the spine on each side stood out rudely, refusing to accept the architect's discipline and discreetly reminding the architect that in structural-shape building the engineer was still the boss in the end.

A few years later Saarinen built another suspended roof from which such visual crudities as these guy wires were eliminated. It was the central terminal at Dulles Airport at Washington, completed after his death in 1962. Its giant roof took the form of a single simple catenary concrete drape between massive angled supports. It was one of the most successful of his works, and one of the best of tensile buildings to this date. Its great strong arms were stretched wide in an innocent gesture seeming to say to the visitor: 'Aren't all airport terminals built like this?' In this respect it was so very different from Saarinen's work of the fifties. Its direct, reasonable, inevitable air put it back, despite its curves and symmetry, into the International Style and the company of Saarinen's early works.

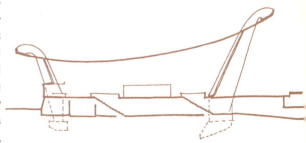

Section through the Dulles terminal

T.W.A. airport terminal

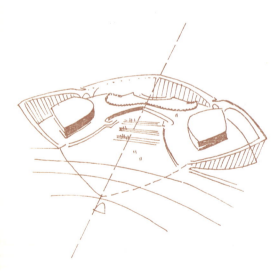

Model with roof removed

In the meantime Saarinen built his most ambitious creation and one which may symbolize the fearless, muddle-headed fifties. It was another exciting shape—the most exciting ever—and in designing it Saarinen changed his standpoint once again. The problem this time was the T.W.A. air terminal building at Kennedy Airport, New York. He made of it the famous giant bird.

Function fitted into the bird. The structure was respected and appears in the finished building quite dominant and convincing. But the design stimulus was no longer intellectual-geometrical or functional-structural. It was architectural-sculptural. Eero Saarinen had a guide vision in his mind from the very start of scrabbling: a free-flowing space with a sense of movement. He did not seek the external bird shape; this was not simply sculpture. He was still an architect first and he sculpted the interior space first, working from the inside out to finish almost accidentally with the bird. The design team worked in three-dimensions, modelling again against a centre-line mirror that made each arbitrary movement symmetrical and to this extent architectonic. Saarinen said at the time that the key to the design was the 'drama of flight and the excitement of travel', as well as the sense of movement which is an intrinsic part of any terminal. All of this he wanted to show in the building itself. After weeks of work in front of the mirror he satisfied himself in shaping a large model to give a visual effect of flow, coinciding generally with the passengers' bodily movement through the building. It is true that some awkward pockets were secreted around the rectilinear services, and the ghost of the model-making mirror lingered on in the kinks which nearly every element suffered at the centre-line. But the space created was powerful and impressive enough to engulf the visitor and flood away concern for some of these disturbing details. Saarinen was too experienced a professional man by this time to allow the difficulties to show. The building worked. The curves were not exciting at the expense of convenience. The great bird did not raise the question of the reasonableness of curved design. After all, rectilinear design is no guarantee of reasonableness. The irregular building is victim to much more searching and even spiteful scrutiny, but there is no inherent reason why a flowing shape should be less functional than a square one—on the contrary it might be more so, in view of human shape.

The puzzle that faced Saarinen and all who followed him in the search for sculptural expression in architecture is not the comparatively simple matter of mastering the technique of bending functional and structural requirements with acceptable logic. After that, after the technique or language is mastered, what have they of value to say that cannot be better said in sculpture?

It is unfair to Saarinen's memory to suggest that he made it bird-shaped deliberately, that he started with a birdlike vision, but perhaps this ambitious man, searching for 'significant form', was not at first distressed too much by the analogy. For, even though the form came from the inside, this was rich man's Mendelsohn—the Expressionism of Erich Mendelsohn's European paper dreams brought to spectacular, even glamorous, American life. Saarinen's giant bird was a fitting climax to the 1950s, the decade of the great shapes. It was conceived with brilliance and executed with masterly professional skill. It was no faltering, isolated experiment, but the end product of a strong branch movement, as polished in its own way as any end product of a movement: say, St Paul's Cathedral or the United Nations Secretariat. It was exciting in shape and structure, and monolithically unified in form. It had no obvious functional flaws nor structural difficulties. It lacked nothing in care, love or money. It summed up the aspirations of the restless fifties: to build with all the expressive fervour of the past but using all the technological resources of the twentieth century. Or, to be plainer, to add poetry to the International Style. And it was a terrible failure. The sad thing was that Saarinen himself knew this before he had finished it, although the sadness was dispelled by the unlikely good luck of a second commission for an airport—the Dulles at Washington—enabling him to reconsider the whole problem in the light of his experience.

The giant bird was a failure for several reasons. For one thing there was something wrong with the scale. In the original model, the drawings, and the descriptions, a building of larger size was suggested, one in which the curves would have sufficient room to float around the functional necessities. For another, the setting could hardly have been less sympathetic. The poor bird was

hemmed in by the utilitarian trappings of a busy airport. It had stolidly rectilinear buildings as close neighbours, which seemed to rebuke it for making so much of a routine problem. Even inside the bird, when the environment was forgotten, the impression of colossal contrivance remained, and the space was always haunted by the ghost of the mirror around which it had been modelled.

Even if the setting and the scale had been right, even if the whole operation had gone as well as Saarinen no doubt dreamt it would in the moment when the vision came to him out of the puzzle pieces, even if it had been perfectly made, still the giant bird would not have been good architecture. For the Mendelsohn dreams do not make sense in real life. It was not the reality of the terminal that led Saarinen to these curves, but, as he said, the movement of the crowd. His curves and swirls symbolized the movement of people on the ground and of planes on the tarmac, just as the external image symbolized flight. It was all advertising of a very high level. It had no reference to the appropriateness of the enclosure as experienced by an occupant. If curves and swirls really do convey a feeling of movement, rather than merely one of restlessness, then the T.W.A. building could be called appropriate symbolically. But no symbol has much connection with the reality. A feeling of movement is not a genuine reflection of the average passenger's emotional state when waiting for his flight signal. Most of us, on the contrary, are conscious of a feeling of excessive stationariness, and impatience, and concern in case we have missed the signal. The architectural expression would have been more valuable if it had adjusted to this state. For ultimate satisfaction with any building is achieved only when the emotional reaction is singular and appropriate to the human experience involved in the activities being housed.

Thus Saarinen, the bright star, brought the era of clear visions and great shapes to a close. This is not to say that grand gestures and succinct shapes will not appear again. Of course they will, but they will never be quite as free again after the lesson of the giant bird, and they will be confined to the simpler functions. Architects in future will be inclined to think again when a giant bird or a cylinder or any other stunningly concise form begins to emerge during the process of scrabbling the programme pieces. At this point an architect of the second phase would become excited, and would encourage the circle and direct everything to that end. But now something inside the architect will begin to warn him when the circle begins to form: he will start to see the pitfalls, the blank panels painted to simulate glass, all the other unrealistic devices that might be necessary finally to contain everything in the circle. He will lead the concept away from the seductive shape and will look for some other solution, something between the loose but practical forms of the first phase and the visually defined but inflexibly tight forms of the second phase. The search will be new with each problem. The aim will be an intense unity without forcing diverse functions into some ill-fitting envelope or an over-rigid pattern, some unreal container. It was the unreal feeling of the giant bird and most of the circles that finally led to their eclipse. Inside the bird, beneath the ghost of the composing mirror, one was merely in the centre of a clever advertisement for air travel, no more real than Gothic Revival; and gradually an impatience with such unreality began to stir architecture again. A longing for more genuine down-to-earthiness came to the surface and in the process submerged most of the feeling for any facile visual delights. This meant the beginning of the end, not only for the exciting sculptural and structural shapes, but also for all aestheticism: for the Yama-saki Gothic Revival and the beautiful grillework of the decorated branch of the second phase. Architecture began to tire of so many pretty things, so many stunning effects. It began to reach out again to try to touch the sterner realities of building.

Part Four | SOLUTIONS

Whatever the limitations of the second phase of modern architecture, the monolithic and engineered shapes together made an important contribution to twentieth-century architecture: the restoration of artistic unity in reaction to loose diagrammatic Functionalism. Yet their limitations were clear enough to many people even at the time, and the paint was not dry on the later examples of monolithism before a new development in another quarter was apparent. This acknowledged the desire for intense unification of the design but tried to find a more flexible method of achieving it. At the same time the new development was resolutely *avant-garde* in spirit; that is, it had every intention of finding a new aesthetic vision while solving the problem.

During the many years since Le Corbusier demonstrated the excitement of levitation in the Villa Savoye, the elevation of mass had been an aesthetic staple, a major part of the generic vision of a twentieth-century style, like the portico of a classical building or the spire of a Gothic cathedral. It was part of the architectural language of the second quarter of the century. When he first viewed the pieces of a client's puzzle, an architect was inclined to look for reasons for raising the building one storey high above the ground. If sufficient excuse could not be found, at least the ground floor front might be recessed a few feet and coloured in a dark shadow tone, in the hope that it might thus disappear.

Now, forty years after the Villa Savoye, levitation had lost its novelty value and its excitement. The very character of lightness, of insubstantiality, of propensity to fly, was losing its charm. For a number of years it had been apparent that the first half of the century, exciting and vital as it might have been at the time, had left very few, if any, monuments. A desire for permanence and monumentality grew in the *avant-garde* studios, and levitation and lightness were recognized as having hindered the development of a monumental look in the new language. At the same time the Mies idiom was losing its enchantment in commercial mass-production. The attraction of blind masonry and brute concrete were recognized again and glass suddenly looked merely fragile and temporary. Recent attempts to beautify the glass curtain with frills, and with arcades at ground level, were edging more serious architects into a position of antagonism to shallow visual attractiveness. While most of them were still not inclined to adopt the heroic pose of the Brutalists and many firmly rejected the crudeness of the more self-consciously rebellious Brutalism, still a number of architects often felt a great sympathy with the strength and decisiveness of the Brutalists. They felt drawn back, morally and logically, to a large part of the theories of spartan simplicity and honesty for which the early twentieth-century pioneers had crusaded, especially the honesty of exposing real, functioning parts of a building instead of packaging them in an exciting shape, or a grille. At the crucial moment in 1960, Louis Kahn, a brilliant Estonian-born American, from whom the world had hitherto heard little although he was sixty, built the Richards Medical Laboratories in Philadelphia.

All at once architecture had a new guide vision. Kahn's laboratories crystallized the several influences that had been growing coincidentally towards the end of the 1950 decade. Some of these influences were old, born with the century, and some were handed on from the other restless sub-movements of the fifties. Thus the new emphasis on wholeness, singleness, or monolithic form, was tempered by a return to the old regard for functional flexibility. The new reaction against lightness and the return to monumentality was allied to the old belief in calling an architectural spade a spade. To men in this partially revolutionary, slightly conservative mood, the Louis Kahn laboratories shone as a sunburst of revelation. The building was without question a single thing, a whole thing, like a grape-bunch building, but more free and apparently functional than any previous bunch. The grapes were different. Kahn separated the functions of the building into two categories: servant and served—as Reyner Banham called them—and made the latter, the laboratories, fragile glass boxes and the former, the mechanical service ducts, hefty workmanlike brick piers. These piers were placed outside the regular square pattern of the glass laboratory walls, in a logical, regular, but not mechanical rhythm. They were great blind straight square brick towers rising from a firm footing in the ground to twenty feet or so above the roof of the laboratories. The towers broke up the glass, cutting it down from big expanses to comparatively small corner cubicles, until the blind towers and glass walls acquired comparable scale in the whole. Kahn achieved artistically a mixture in which everything of relevance

Richards Medical Laboratories

132

to the job in hand—but nothing more—could be seen fragmented, naked and identifiable, while no single element dominated and all were subordinated to the total thing.

Mechanical services had been exposed before this. In a conference room at United Nations for instance, Sven Markelius, desperate for a constructive idea to bring to an impossible interior-decoration commission which he had been given as a political sop, left off the usual false ceiling and painted the plumber's jungle in bright colours. The Smithsons and other Brutalists in England ran electrical conduits on the surface of walls. But Louis Kahn's clever idea was different. He did not merely admit the presence of the mechanical services. In this laboratory building which depended so greatly on mechanisms and ductwork, he proclaimed, paraded and publicly honoured the pipes and the toxic fumes in monumental pylons. The easy logic of this bright and honest thought attracted a generation which was having increasing difficulty in hiding the growing volume of mechanical services. Here was a delightful twist: if architecture could not fight the services, it must join them.

There were serious critics of the building who claimed that the monumental duct-pylons were more for show than for use, or at least a lot bigger than they need have been, and there were other services in the building which eluded the enormous pylons and went their way unhonoured. On the other hand, here was a monument achieved within the rational code. Here was a single unified thing, yet one which clearly followed some functional programme in its erratic external form, which was transparently honest and true to the spirit of the mechanized laboratories which it served. Moreover it was as exciting visually as a cylinder or a bird.

The visual excitement of Kahn's laboratories came partially from the grape-bunch-style repetition of elements, but more importantly from the complex massing of the whole. In a sense Kahn turned the twentieth-century space concept inside out. In the standard Miesian vernacular building the exterior was as close as possible to a bland cube but the interior permitted itself a little non-geometrical play with space—the asymmetrical, teasing, unrevealed, multi-level space of the century. For instance, inside a clear, clean, modularly organized room a screen or smaller block room might be placed deliberately off-centre. Mies himself was prepared to spend a lot of time on determining the exact proportions of such deliberate interruptions to his pristine open spaces. However, while the Kahn laboratories were not of great spatial interest internally, the same sort of inconsequential, sensitively haphazard interruptions broke the space immediately around the building. It was always the same single thing as one walked around it, yet it changed continuously, promising more, half-revealing yet half-hiding the next wing. Here was promise, on top of all the other attractions, of a new exterior excitement to relieve the monotony of the glass cubes and the geometrical sterility of the monolithic monument.

Thus the Kahn laboratories formed the next new generic guide vision, and all over the world, perhaps nowhere more than in England, the random pylon look was presented to clients who wanted schools, motels, factories, colleges and even houses, and who had never heard of Louis Kahn. In January 1961 the design for a memorial in Washington to Franklin Delano Roosevelt was selected by competition. It consisted of eight enormous slabs or pylons, the tallest reaching 167 feet, the shortest about a quarter of that height, all set at random levels and angles to each other, but consistent in their proportions, verticality and shape. It was planned to involve the pedestrian spectator in a series of 'memorable open-ended spatial sequences'. It was thus the first pure monument of the third phase of modern architecture, and an exact style symbol of its time. It was not, however, approved by the Fine Arts Commission, and its architects—Pedersen, Tilney, Hoberman, Wasserman and Beer—were asked to redesign it. They made it more acceptable, though still not to the liking of the Roosevelt family, by reducing the height of the pylons and bringing some order to their random arrangement, and by placing a larger-than-life statue of Roosevelt at a focal point; in short, by retreating to a first-phase solution.

Nevertheless on occasions less charged with emotional and artistic stress, the bold block pylons continued their random advance. They seldom housed ducts any more, but they often took stairs and elevators and other central services. Suddenly it seemed that all such services had to be pulled like periwinkles from the insides of their buildings and erected separately along-

Design for F.D.R. memorial, rejected

side. This device frequently had practical advantages, but the random pylon effect was also adopted at times quite arbitrarily and meaninglessly without any relevance to the plan. Thus transferred to a visual fashion the random pylons soon palled, and were dropped, but in the meantime they had broken the strength of the monolithic vision.

Now a reaction against the elegant finishes of the second phase appeared. In the 1930s, during the honeymoon of architecture and the machine, the European leaders, including Mies van der Rohe and Le Corbusier, were fascinated with precision, polish and minimum tolerances, with chromium-plated steel, aluminium, and dry composites. After 1945 Mies took this approach to the U.S.A. and found for the first time a technology that would respond to his most exacting demands. Under the Mies influence in most of the western world both serious architecture and commercial building had in common the technical aims of precision, hard, true edges, and high polish. The more general this became, the more Wright, Le Corbusier, and some others, deplored it. Wright clung to his cottage-style finishes: warm wood, brown stonework, sandy plaster, avoiding as he said 'the pessimistic blues of the ribbon counter'. When he used concrete he set big rocks in it like nuts in chocolate, as in his home in Arizona called Taliesin West, or he rendered it over in sandy plaster, as in his greatest house, Fallingwater, or his last major work, the Guggenheim Museum. In either case he was intent on softening the hard, cold nature of concrete. Le Corbusier, on the contrary, was delighted with the look of the solid grey mass imprinted with the grain and joints of the timber in which it was formed. He loved the rugged might of it and despised the effete elegance in the dapper details of more commercial architects' work. He departed as far as Wright did from an engineer's optimum design for concrete, but in the opposite direction, away from cosiness to tame brute strength. The Japanese, who recognized Le Corbusier only among the western leaders, adopted a similar gargantuan technique with concrete. Grey, grained and overweight, it was the defiant, rude reply to the shibui, shoji, tatami tradition by the creative architects of new Japan. The British Brutalists admired the strength of concrete as much as anyone, but traditionally and economically were bound more to brickwork, which nevertheless

Fallingwater, at Bear Run, Pennsylvania

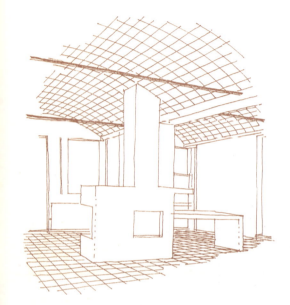

Le Corbusier's Maisons Jaoul at Neuilly

could look almost equally rugged if the joints were treated with vigour and the pointing iron were spared. The building of Le Corbusier which most influenced them, and which formed the main guide vision for Brutalists, was the Maisons Jaoul at Neuilly, built in 1952. This pair of houses mixed panels of raw brickwork, and vaults and floors of earthenware tiles, with heavy horizontal bands of stripped concrete. In California and Australia, where timber remained the most convenient material for smaller buildings, the reaction against elegance was manifested occasionally in rough sawn lumber, spared the agony of the plane.

All this tinkering with technique was symptomatic of a new impatience with the old love of the machine. It was a modest step in the direction of a return to primitivity or fundamentalism in design. The trancendental or cosmic concept of architecture, never far beneath the surface of dedicated architects' thought, was overcoming the temporary fascination with the machine and pleasing forms.

' "*Pleasing form" alone is nothing. We are not a group of artists. "Building" stands above all artistry. It is the vast arc encompassing everything. And out of it all, spontaneously, the great Form will be born as if generated of itself.*' These words of Bruno Taut addressed to his unemployed architect friends in the depressed Berlin of 1920 in no way exaggerate a feeling shared by many who come under the spell of architecture's power. Architects are granted the ability to control the shape of civilization. Thus, 'We are God', pronounced a leader writer in a Melbourne architectural students' journal of 1950, rather losing his head.

Ordinary architectural practice is a dull business of keeping costs down, weather out, and clients and builders from each other's throats. Nevertheless a great number of architects retain from student enthusiasms a religious devotion to the concept of architecture as the 'vast arc' beside which any other expressions of mankind are like scribbles in the dust. To realize its magnificent destiny architecture must, of course, rise above petty considerations of day-to-day problems and find a new plane where concepts flood in with the light of the sun, free of all associations with previous architecture or with any other works of man. The glorious idea of a pure transcendant architecture tends to get beaten out of the brain of the average practitioner as the real work of administering modern building operations engulfs him. It could not be farther from the aim of most men for whom he is building, who want only to acquire an economical, comfortable, saleable structure. Bruno Taut's attitude to this conflict of aim was clear. 'I find clients almost repulsive', he wrote.

The transcendental view of architecture appears through the ages, but as an active movement it is only about as old as modern architecture. It grew out of some of the same foundations: the flexibility and scale of the new engineering and the sense of glorious freedom after the historical apron strings were broken. It associated itself with the central modern development, although this attachment was not always reciprocated.

The manifestations of Transcendentalism fell generally into two categories. One was almost literally the 'vast arc', a huge enclosure of some pure and simple form in which one created a little Utopia or Garden of Eden. The geodesic domes of Buckminster Fuller typify this kind. Fuller sees whole cities enclosed by plastic domes, enjoying a perpetual artificial spring. As an engineer, Fuller's dreams are a little more concrete and less poetic than the architectural Transcendentalists, but he has the necessary enthusiasm and fundamentalism.

'Do you remember as a child', he was quoted by a *Time* writer in January 1964, 'what it was like playing house out in the woods? It was exciting. It was wonderful—until it rained. Well, I could build you that house today, where the sunlight would come through just as in the forest. A house with no walls, no doors, no windows—only paths of green ferns and green trees through a rainbow of flowers. And it would never rain. I call this house "The Garden of Eden".' In this kind of Utopia an enclosing balloon was necessary for practical reasons, to confine the volume to be air-conditioned and to keep out the rain. But it was to be as transparent and invisible as possible. Fuller's idea was to make it of two dome frameworks, the outer one encouraging vines and the inner one plasticized to keep out the rain. The Fuller dome was indeed the most practical of the vast arcs ever proposed and it has, of course, many commercial and industrial applications which have been fairly thoroughly investigated and exploited. Its potentialities in the cause of transcendental archi-tecture have hardly been tested, although George Nelson and

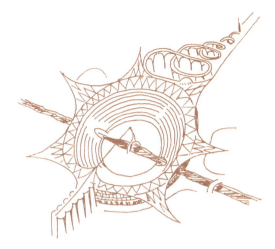

Bruno Taut's design for a community centre

Buckminster Fuller's geodesic dome structure

137

other designers have indicated how a house of the future, utilizing a Fuller dome, might look like a giant soap bubble enclosing, with an almost accidental air, a section of one's garden. Inside, screens and platforms, but no walls as such, would be arranged for privacy. The enclosing architectural element, the bubble, would be reduced to a thick film, the minimum necessary to resist collapse in a high wind and to restrict the air-conditioned volume. This idea has never been built, but it has had some influence on conventional building. Numerous houses have cautiously followed the same theme, to the extent that whatever artistic qualities they have are confined to the subdivision and continuity of the enclosed space, while the enclosing envelope is played down as far as possible towards the desired end of invisibility. On the other hand, the proposals by Frei Otto for tension structures and pneumatic envelopes leave the Fuller domes behind in the realm of conventional building.

The other category of transcendental architecture shuns the transparency and extroversion of the vast arc school, but it is no less fundamental in attitude. It seeks to take man back to the earth, or the womb. For several years in Mozambique the architect Amancio d'Aboim Guedes has specialized in free-formed, soft moulded concrete, making, as he says, 'swollen houses out on a manhunt for themselves'. He has designed a house he calls 'The Habitable Woman'. It is, he explains with his tongue not entirely in his cheek, 'an anthropomorphic wonder-house . . . a round-eyed house of cavernous passages built into the rock gaps, of swinging walls finding their own levels, of fluid ceilings and floors, of many stairs and steps, with lights staring and pouncing out of ceilings and walls; a house with a baby-house inside her. A pregnant building. A doll's house with secret and hanging gardens. My most hysterical construction.' Again, the 'Endless House', a design of 1960 by Frederick J. Kiesler, looks in plan or in the round like a lumpy bread roll. Some of the lumps are bedrooms and some sitting-rooms or a kitchen. But there are no conventional doors between any of them, only a slight constriction of space at the more private portals. The whole is moulded out of concrete; floors, walls and roof blending into one. 'The form of The Endless House is not a free-flow art form, as many suspect', insists its architect, 'but derives from living a life

The Habitable Woman

dedicated to fundamentals rather than to mechanized equipment and interior decoration, or to a return to primitivity.' This concept has been carried to commercial success by Jacques Conelle in a snobby sub-division of womb houses at Castellaras-le-Neuf on the French Riviera. 'The floor of the building can be level', says Conelle, 'but all the rest must be movement. I am disgusted with architecture. My dream is to make an abode of instinct, like an animal's.'

This second kind of Trancendentalism, then, turns into itself, and is more modest in intention and scale. Yet is it no less proud, wilfully independent of all that has gone before, and Utopian in spirit. Both categories of Transcendentalist architect are inclined to see themselves as the only architects who are attempting to create real architecture. They look with scorn on the superficial visual effects of most of their colleagues, and are almost equally contemptuous of the pedestrian work that they themselves are forced to do by those repulsive clients.

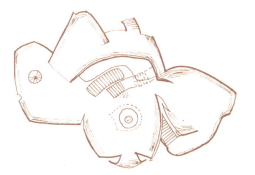

The Endless House

So much had happened since 1950, so many new shapes and techniques and surface treatments had been devised, that the modern movement may have seemed, in the early 1960s, to be bursting with creative vigour. Yet those many effects and fashions really had much in common with each other and more in common with the Victorians than their supporters were prepared to admit. For underneath the sophisticated technology and the newer, more whimsical ways of pilfering from history, nearly all the twentieth century's architecture to this time was still essentially an art of composition: the arranging of structural, useful and decorative elements to create pleasing effects. This description fitted not only the frankly ingratiating buildings which wrapped themselves around with grilles and pointed arcades, but also the masses of blind masonry and brute concrete which were defiantly, arrogantly non-pleasing to the uninitiated. In fact the spirit of twentieth-century architecture was by no means satisfied yet. The revolution of the Transcendentalists was always simmering, fundamentally rebellious, subversive to the traditional object of architecture to create beautiful buildings. Its cause was always Utopian: the creation of perfect living space, which was quite a different thing from the erection of beautiful solids.

Not all extraordinary, imaginary or visionary architecture comes within the transcendental category. In slack moments students and enthusiasts are liable to conceive fantastic towers, twisted domes and grottoes, which may be impossible to build and meaningless if built. But all the strange underground movements, burrowing for the very heart of architecture, are not to be derided too lightly. 'A beautiful idea in embryo has in it something absurd for fools' said Debussy, and Bruce Goff, one of the very few Transcendentalists who has made a respectable career without compromising, likes to quote him.

Individual attempts to construct Utopian spaces with mundane building-trade resources have led in the past to a number of buildings like Goff's Bavinger house, which are so strange as to be classed by most people as more or less crackpot, and thus dismissed. Mendelsohn was in his early days a Transcendentalist, but he had not the technical resources available or at his command and had to build the Einstein Tower out of dull brickwork with the corners knocked off to give a plastic continuity in the final plastered form. Naturally such irrational compromises discredited the Transcendentalists. Bruce Goff's Bavinger house would be acceptable to only one family in a thousand, and half of them would be more moved by the notoriety than the feeling that, despite the discomfort, they were reaching uncertainly towards Utopia.

The Transcendentalist architect is a conceptualist, whole hog. He takes the central step, the conceptual step of design, as the only really important one and he concentrates on this to such an extent that the other two usually suffer. He sometimes asks others to look after these for him, with predictable results. Almost every architect would like to be a Transcendentalist architect whose buildings worked—'worked' meaning worked for ordinary decent clean-thinking people. Unfortunately this is impossible, since to work for the mass is by definition not to transcend. Thus ordinary workaday architects rather bitterly accuse anyone attempting to transcend as being extremist, of going too far. But Bruce Goff replies: 'What real artists ever went too far, when judged from the perspective of later years? We usually wish that they had gone further.'

Nevertheless the Utopian space concept has remained more or less a joke in the eye of the public, or that section of the public which has heard of it. The Bavinger house, with its spiral form and hanging saucers, typified the potential laughing stock. Its external appearance was indeed close to slapstick, with its incoherent twists of roofing metal, suspension wires, rubble stonework, rustic mullions and bits of glass; but the joke was temporary and did not reduce the importance of this strange house.

One of the incidental effects of the engineers' work on shell concrete and tension structure was to provide buildings as unconventional as the Bavinger house with a rational and appropriate means of construction, rather than a dozen or so different semi-adequate materials which when jointed in painstaking detail managed to stay together tightly enough just to withstand the weather. Shell concrete presented one material, one enclosing idea. Utopia, of course, calls for a single structural idea as it does for an all-embracing flash of inspiration for its character. Tension and other advanced structural methods began in the sixties slowly to catch up with the Transcendentalists, promising to make Utopian space respectable. It was apparent that some day most buildings would be as irregular, in their own ways, as the Bavinger house or the Endless House, but by then their irregularity would be so familiar as to raise no eyebrows. We of the 1960s are in no position to guess at the appearance of the products of later generations. We can be fairly sure that they will not look like anything in our science-fiction, which is based on our present-day technology and our inhibited visual taste. But those future Utopian owners will know if their buildings are good or bad, using the same yardstick that is available to us. They will ask—or rather the architectural critics of their time should ask— are their buildings emotionally satisfying in ways that seem appropriate to the occupiers and their duties and their Utopian delights? For architecture even then will still be nothing if not a useful art and, very literally, a living art, and if the image created is not in accordance realistically with the fragment of life being sheltered, then, whether it is imaginative, visionary, pedestrian or commercial, it will still be bad architecture.

The language of architecture, distinct from the language of painting or sculpture, is the modelling of defined, occupiable space. The Romans and the Goths knew this as well as we do, and each had his own idiom in the spatial language. The most important contribution of the twentieth century to this old art was the freeing of space from centre-lines and symmetry, the playing with space, pursuing it round corners and out of sight behind incomplete partitions. This was the one artistic element common to nearly all the styles of the century. It was neglected only by the more extreme and static Monolithicists of the late 1950s in their concentration on external form. Otherwise it was the one unifying theme of the three phases of modern architecture.

Never forgetting the consistency of this theme, we can see that modern architecture went through a convulsive visual change from the first phase of articulated functional planning to the second phase of monolithic monumentality. Violent changes of this sort are characteristic of architecture, an outward display of the internal stress of an art with two such inconsistent sides: the side of useful technology and the side of expression. The timeless puzzle for the architect is to try to reconcile these inconsistencies, but understandably enough most architects err by leaning temperamentally too far to one side or the other. Each of the first two phases of modern architecture leaned too far, but in opposite directions.

The first phase, the early International and Organic Styles, even at their best when operating as intended, were literally and artistically loose. Their separate parts, proudly displayed and composed, lacked the single visionary quality essential to a compelling expression.

The major reaction to this was, as we have seen, the second phase, of the glass cylinders, wrap-around grilles, monumental monoliths and geometrical-structural forms, into which different functions were stuffed willy-nilly. All such forms to some extent over-simplified the functional problem, but they did serve to remind architecture that a work of art requires unity and singleness of purpose if it is to express anything, to communicate any idea. But in the oversimplification of the problem every building of the second phase ran a risk of looking as shallow as an exposition building: monumental and visionary, but a little too obviously so. So the third phase grew up in a search of another, better, more convincing means of achieving a visionary simplicity. While the first and second phases continue to this day with

142

weakening strength, this third phase seeks to combine the functional freedom and the clear structural and spatial articulation of the first phase with the monumental artistic unity of the second.

The English group which was pleased to be called Brutalist helped to lead the way into the third phase with the strength of its naked structural materials and its heroic stand against any ornament, or any concessions to visual habits. The Japanese, after Le Corbusier, advanced the concept of unity of material. Kenzo Tange's mighty Kurashiki City Hall, designed in 1958 and built in 1960, had an intense unity resulting from a concentration on the single material of concrete, used consistently in giant beams or precast planks. There was a functional freedom in the distribution of the planks, and the glass, somewhere behind the gaps, could not be seen. Overall the building had the massive unarguable conviction of a log cabin, or an igloo.

In La-Tourette monastery and the government centre at Chandigarh in India, Le Corbusier demonstrated with customary assurance how far it was possible to shatter familiar square forms with fragmentary surface treatment and yet hold all the pieces together by a consistently strong personal attack on every problem that arose. However, Louis Kahn most succinctly stated the new aims in popularly understandable terms in his Richards Medical Laboratories, and thus finally turned modern architecure round the corner into the third phase. As this m ovement developed it seemed to be an amalgam of all the most convincing experiences in half a century of modern architecture, and a controlled rather than a compulsive search for the ultimate architectural vision.

Le Corbusier's Congress building at Chandigarh

It was the most sophisticated movement since the industrial revolution, and yet in purely visual terms it was almost conservative, for the search for unity outside geometrical envelopes or rigid repetitive panels often led back over old ground. The critics were quick to notice the resemblance of Paul Rudolph's architecture and art school at Yale to Frank Lloyd Wright's Larkin Building of 1904. Houses by John M. Johansen after 1960 drew the eye back much further, back to a peublo, or a Greek village of cottages burrowing into a white cliff face. The third-phase architects solved the problem of unity most frequently by harmonic shapes: the pylons of Kahn's laboratories, the curved corners of blind concrete walls in Johansen's house overlooking Long Island Sound, the giant free-standing sun visors of Rudolph's beach house near Jacksonville, Florida. Always some theme based on function repeated and repeated, but not monotonously as in a grape-bunch building of the second phase. As in pop paintings or a new-wave film or in much jazz, the element changed with nearly every repetition, sometimes obviously, sometimes almost imperceptibly. But change it did, injecting life into unity. The analogy with other pop art forms of the 1960s is not meant to denigrate the well-publicized buildings mentioned. Inevitably, involuntarily, an alert building will reflect something of the aesthetic mood of its moment and if that mood has a teenage jumpiness at this moment, then alert buildings are bound to be a little jumpy. (They are never, however, literally teenage. Architecture is the one art that has never hailed an infant prodigy. By its nature it grants proper opportunities only to the middle-aged or elderly.) Being contemporary in this sense is hardly the same as being fashionable. In any case varied repetition has the oldest architectural precedents. Variety within unity was Christopher Wren's definition of beauty, and Hogarth's. Repetition with variation was the involuntary technique of peasant builders. Yet in the third phase of modern architecture the unity was more carefully guarded and the variations more consciously developed than in most previous eras of architecture. Each building was a whole peasant village in itself.

Other ways will be found to bring unity to design solutions, other means of expressing a consistent idea so dominating as to suppress any individual element. Artists of the third phase will find new ways by dragging some formal meaning out of the programme of the problem they are studying, while remembering always that their art is concerned with modelling space. The ways already found by Kahn, Rudolph, Johansen, Tange and others are mainly important to the extent that they prove that there are successful ways other than bare simplicity and geometrical regularity to make a firm architectural statement. The architects of the next decade will investigate other ways and may produce the long-anticipated flowering of twentieth-century architecture about 1976. Or, as is perhaps more likely, they will fail to find other ways, and the third phase of modern architecture will subside into a fashion of asymmetry, fragmentation, and further confusion.

Some suggestions of other ways were seen in the early sixties. In one of the most unexpected fields, a mass housing estate called Park Hill at Sheffield, England, a young team under the Sheffield City Architect, J. L. Womersley, produced a fine example of the third phase. It was a slum clearance scheme of vast proportions, nearly a thousand apartments, on a big, sloping, unprepossessing site.

An architect of the first phase might have solved this problem by sorting the different sizes and kinds of accommodation required into categories, then building a rectilinear block for each one, eight or ten of them, varying in height and length as required by the size of flat enclosed. Some squat for families, one or two needle towers for childless people; all varying in window treatment and balcony provisions as required by the rooms. He would have painted all the blocks white, and this might have been the only indication that all of them were part of the one scheme, conceived at the same time.

An architect of the second phase faced with the same problem might have surveyed for some time the sloping site, chin in hand, before deciding that all the flats could be contained in one eight-storey serpentine block, twisting down the hill, a huge S-shape for Sheffield.

The Sheffield team's solution was, unlike the first, a single thing but, unlike the second, a living thing. They planned about twenty blocks connected to each other at their ends but angled variously to form semi-enclosed irregular private courts. Then they tied all the blocks together by a system of narrow elevated streetways, at every third floor level, which sometimes hugged the blocks and sometimes bridged the gaps between them. These elevated streets were intended for social communication and light wheel traffic. The whole was subjected to an irregular but consistent structure of exposed concrete frame and brick panels. Here, then, was a concept based on the human activities while exploring the three dimensions of space.

The great building boom of the early sixties in and around Cambridge, Massachusetts, was dominated by third-phase feeling, largely in the work of Jose Luis Sert, the dean of architecture at

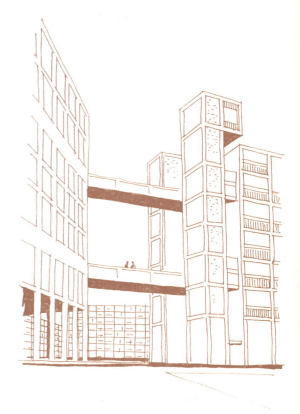

Park Hill apartments at Sheffield

145

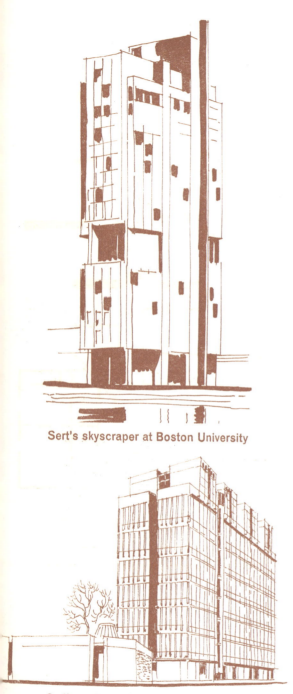

Sert's skyscraper at Boston University

Cadbury-Brown's Royal College of Art

Harvard. In the Holyoke medical centre near Harvard Square he introduced a highly diversified facade of ribbed solids, slit windows, spots of colour and projecting hoods. It was a clear reaction to second-phase monolithic forms, but rather an unconstructive one. In his later blocks of Harvard married-student apartments, completed in 1965, the variations on the exterior were still more pronounced, looked more convincing, and the treatment was more consistent. In the 'vertical campus' of a modest skyscraper for Boston University across the Charles River he combined a law department, education department, library, incinerator shaft and other elements in a strongly modelled block. This was more than frank in its external expression of the various internal activities. A distinct waistline was apparent about a third of the way up the building where the law department stopped and the education department began. Such vigorous external modelling was another way of breaking up the box, the monolith. Sert set upon it, as Le Corbusier had done at Chandigarh, and years earlier at Algiers, but Sert seemed even more impatient with his own box, furiously attacking it. In a comparable building of mixed functions in the same period, the Royal College of Art in London, the architect H. T. Cadbury-Brown also designed a box and then slashed into it from the outside, but in a more reserved, British way.

These men helped to steer architecture towards the third phase, but none of the buildings mentioned quite reached it. They had the essential functional freedom from geometrical rule, and the Royal College of Art, at least, played with space whenever this seemed convenient or possible. Yet they lacked a single-minded driving idea that might have unified the fragments into an expressive whole. Louis Kahn, on the other hand, was one who demonstrated the necessary compulsiveness again and again. Each of his later buildings had some quite simple but apt intellectual idea, usually achieved by long, dogged work over the drawing board and after rejection of more facile preliminary schemes. These ideas were often visually intricate; thus they were essentially different from the succinct spontaneous brainwave concepts of the second phase. A characteristic Kahn idea can be examined in embryo in the sketchy solution he gave to a small problem of 1959, projected while the Philadelphia medical school was still in

146

development. This was the **Goldenberg** house. It was planned with rooms around an exactly square courtyard, which is a concept as old as the hills and a favourite device of the second phase, as in Stone's New Delhi Embassy. Louis Kahn, however, rejuvenated and transformed it by liberating the surrounding rooms from the geometrical bondage of the square. Each room or space was permitted to expand to the size required by its own function, observing only the diagonal extensions of the square and breaking through the perimeter. Each room thus took a size and shape which was 'what it wanted to be', as Louis Kahn puts it. The house exploded outwards and took on a new, integrated but irregular form. It was still a formal idea, yet one free from the embarrassments of the closed forms of second-phase design. In such a scheme Kahn could hardly be forced into a dilemma of choice during the design development between conflicting formal and functional requirements. The living spaces could grow or deflate as required without disturbing the formal concept.

These buildings were almost desperately exploiting the third dimension in an attempt to reach a richer architecture. The most important thing about the third phase was the way that it returned for artistic expression to the heart of the architectural medium: to negative form, or space. Not merely the internal, enclosed space, but the half-enclosed and the half-exposed. After all the laughter and tears shed over the search for significant solid form, architects were coming back home to the heart of their medium, They remembered the early Wright. They remembered the essence of the Giedion thesis.

Sigfried Giedion's monumental history of the birth and development of twentieth-century architecture was published first in 1941 and ran through five editions before the end of World War II. It was subtitled 'The growth of a new tradition' and it helped to consolidate that tradition as building began slowly to recover after the war. No doubt it would have been a successful book even without its romantic title, *Space, Time and Architecture*. With the assistance of the intellectually flattering, science-fiction fascination of that title the book became the gospel of the first post-war generation of architects. Giedion traced the origins of modern architectural space themes from the perspectives of the

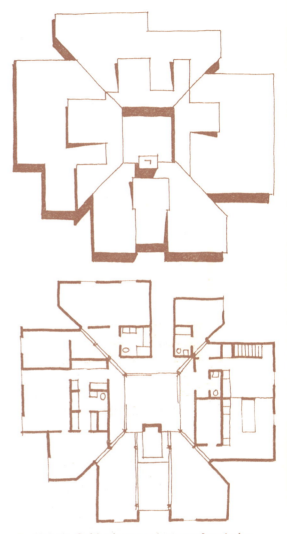

Kahn's Goldenberg project: roof and plan

147

Renaissance through the plaster sunbursts of the Baroque and the vast exhibition halls made possible by steel in the Victorian era to the hide-and-seek spaces of the first half of the twentieth century. Giedion also glorified the austere white style in which these later spaces were wrapped. In the 1960s a new star critic, Vincent Scully Jr of Yale University, exposed flaws in the older man's argument, but nothing would erase the influence of Giedion's emphasis on space during the impressionable post-war period.

A mystique then surrounded the word space, and this was not to decline as space travel and space consciousness came out of science-fiction into the daily news of the next decade. A good deal of pseudo-scientific reference entered the vocabulary of some architectural critics and students about 1950. 'Spatial interpenetration' was a favourite way of describing the effect when nothing more than a large opening was made between two rooms. The enthusiastic architects who had been restrained from building through the war years somehow saw a link between the dark infinity of cosmic space and the removal of old barriers to continuous space between their living-room, dining-room and kitchen. Yet despite the excesses of language and the incautious destruction of privacy in the 1950s, despite a lot of nonsense written around space, the fact remains beyond all argument that the shaping of enclosed living space is the one essential that distinguishes architecture from the other arts and crafts. The first phase of modern architecture was always prepared to remember this. The second was inclined to forget it while concentrating on the shaping of some succinct solid mass.

When a first-phase architect regarded the long history of his art, his interest gravitated to the periods with the richest play or patterns of interior spaces: to the Gothic cathedrals and the Baroque churches and palaces. Architects of the second phase were more interested in the concise monuments: the Parthenon, and the Doge's Palace at Venice.

At Agra, India, a first-phase tourist would spend most time examining the intricacies of the courtyards, loggias and semi-open chambers of the Red Fort, while his second-phase friend admired the Taj Mahal across the Jumna River. To the first-phase man the Taj was in itself no more than a glorious giant

148

jewel box, or mammoth formal sculpture. It was architecture only in the context of its attendant buildings within the high red sandstone boundary wall.

The Taj Mahal greatly moved the second-phase man emotionally when he visited it at night, when it was isolated, white and almost transparent against the stars. But by day, brilliantly in command of its great perspective of pools and minarets, it meant most to the first-phase man, who chose to examine it as he first came upon it, framed by the opening in the great dark sandstone entrance gateway, linked to other spaces, and to life rather than death.

This is not to suggest that the architects of the second phase always ignored the interior spaces. On the contrary, the best examples were as well balanced, inside to outside, as the best architecture of any era. Stone conceived the New Delhi Embassy as a hollow form, the interior courtyard pool and awning being a sort of negative version of the exterior concept. Saarinen began shaping the T.W.A. terminal internally, and spent more time on the interior shapes. The giant bird form grew almost unnoticed and inadvertently around him.

One of Philip Johnson's most personal and delightful buildings, the Dumbarton Oaks museum near Washington, demonstrated splendidly both pure second-phase design and how to have fun with space. It was a folly, a garden ornament, a small pavilion of extraordinary richness for this century, made to exhibit a few dozen pieces of Pre-Columbian art. An exemplar of brain-wave design, its plan consisted of nine circles stacked into a square, three rows of three, with the centre one removed to form an open space. The theme of the circle permeated everywhere. There were no walls as such, but rich plump cylindrical columns and curved glass walls. Each of the eight circular cells was roofed with its own little dome. It was perhaps the least functional building erected since the Albert Memorial, and as full of wanton delights, but delights of this century. The sense of interior space was intimate, unique and appropriate to the exquisite and sumptuous nature of the project. The space did not flow so much as it pranced elegantly from one cell to the next, and hopped in and out of the humanly-inaccessible central court where a heavy jet of water spilled over black stones. This

Johnson's Dumbarton Oaks museum

was witty space, but at the same time as courtly and formal as the exterior of any second-phase building.

The architects of the third phase, in breaking from nutshell concepts, renounced all such formalities and sought freer expressions in space, and stronger ones. So much had been said and written about spatial flow and interpenetration and contrast, but so little really had been ventured. No architectural study had been made of the psychological consequences of spaces, of claustrophobia, vertigo, agoraphobia, or the difference in people's heads for heights. Could these and other human reactions to spaces be ordered into some sort of scale? If so, perhaps architects could then better understand what they do to their occupants when they alter ceiling heights and floor levels, and when they present people with potential death drops just outside sheets of glass.

Unfamiliar experiences in space were largely responsible for the sensation caused by Paul Rudolph's school of architecture and art at Yale in 1964. This 'furiously ambitious building', as Professor Vincent Scully called it, combined nearly all the qualities sought in the third phase. It had a strong sense of emotional freedom and yet every element in it was intellectually conceived. It was fragmented and bursting with vitality and yet it was a single thing, indivisible and complete. A rigid consistency ran through the hand-textured ribbed concrete of the vertical supports and the plain stripped beams. But the most important of all the elements in which it worked was space. This was the essence of all its effects.

The intellectual control of this building began when Rudolph determined its height and overall mass before he started to design. He did this out of neighbourliness—to Albert Kahn's Fine Arts Gallery on the opposite corner, and even to the very ordinary old commercial buildings beside it on busy Chapel Street. The plan form has been described as pinwheel. It does have a certain rotational feeling which was deliberate, to carry the eye and the street around the corner. It is dominated by a number of blind piers, or towers, some of which stop short of the top while others break the skyline. The floors are like trays spanning between these pylons on four perimeters, leaving space in the centre. The trays are at random if not arbitrary levels. The space in the centre

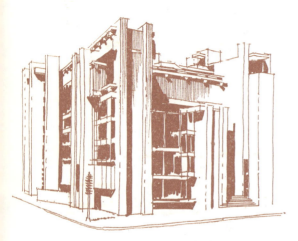

School of architecture and art at Yale

is largely occupied by the tall jury room and exhibition area of the architecture department. This is the spatial heart of the building. The shallow trays of the drawing studios surround it and overlook it. Classrooms, library and offices are half-open to it behind the grey ribbed concrete piers. Open shafts rise above through upper floors to skylights. A narrow bridge spans between trays through mid space.

The likeness to Frank Lloyd Wright's early Larkin Building is undeniable, but the unlikenesses are more significant. The Larkin Building also had a lofty internal volume overlooked by 'trays' or open floors of normal height offices. But the Larkin space was modular, regular, made to a pattern which, once stated on the first level, repeated predictably up the three further floors. Rudolph's spaces are unpredictable, while the masses that form them remain disciplined and consistent. A final touch in the spatial design, but the first device to meet the visitor, is the arrangement of the entrance, up a flight of steps in a slit between two towering monoliths. It is like entering a gold mine at the bottom.

The thunderously impressive control of space in this building did not excuse its many impractical elements in the eyes of many people, including Nikolaus Pevsner, who was invited to open it. It had no privacy, even for the Dean, its architect, in his own office. The artists and sculptors bitterly criticized the low ceilings of their sections. It is inadequately ventilated and sun-screened for a building which does not enjoy air-conditioning. Yet these are practical oversights of an architect who had an indulgent client, himself, rather than failure of the principle of functional design, and they should distract no one from understanding that this was a building which tried to claw its way back into the very heart of architecture.

In Japan at about the same time Kenzo Tange was feeling his way forward and backward into new adventures in space. Tange's is a brilliant talent and the new Japan has given it fertile ground. He began his meteoric career by winning a competition for the Hiroshima Peace Memorial in 1949 at the age of thirty-six. The completed memorial immediately demonstrated his potential powers. It had the strength and dignity essential to its terrible function. It was a long, low, elevated concrete box with deep

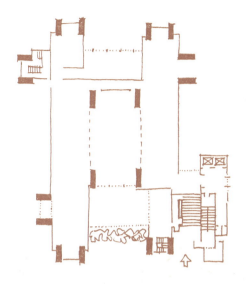

Plan and section of the school at Yale

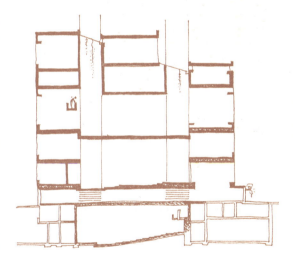

concrete fins protecting its glass. It was subsequently flanked by two other Tange designs that were even more clearly mono-lithic in concept. They were squares containing the hotel, audi-torium, and a community centre. But the memorial itself was not categorical second phase. It had an irregular structural frame, and although its deep window mullions observed a module they missed a half beat at each irregular bay of the structure. This practical and subtle variation gave vitality to what might otherwise have been a monotonous and inadequate statement.

Tange went on to build several good examples of the second phase in the next few years: nutshell concepts like the Ehime Convention Centre of 1952, under a dome, and the square, bal-cony-ringed tower of the Kagawa Prefectural Government Office in 1955. Nearly always there was something of a rebellious irregu-larity around the fringes of his ideas, and his Kurashiki City Hall of 1960 was a decisive break with monolithic concepts. It had a regular plan of three giant bays, each about sixty feet wide. Each side bay held three storeys of offices, but this could not be seen from the outside, because floor lines were lost behind the wall treatment. For most of the facade this consisted, as we have seen, of an assemblage of concrete planks, sometimes close together and sometimes irregularly spaced apart. In places the slits between planks partially revealed windows set back some inches inside, but in effect nothing other than the concrete could be seen. The planks were sharply cut, and their ends at corners of the buildings were deliberately out of line, as if carelessly erected, to accentuate their separateness. It looked elemental and innocent and free, and yet at the same time rigidly disciplined by the clearly displayed massive structure, and held in sub-mission by the vice-like grip of enormous concrete beams at top and bottom, spanning the sixty-feet bays. Here, then, was consistency and coherence, with irregularity and apparent functional freedom. It was a firm step into the third phase. It even had a spatial climax like a drum-roll in the huge central area, the public waiting hall, which was conceived by Tange at the 'mass-human scale', as he describes it.

Impressive as was this vast hollow in the centre of the build-ing, it added little but size to architectural understanding of space. But in another project of the same period Kenzo Tange pursued

Kurashiki City Hall

the dramatic qualities of space into much more subtle volumes. This project was his unsolicited plan for Tokyo published magnanimously in 1960. His solution to the problems of congestion and visual confusion in the world's biggest city was to build out across Tokyo Bay. In order to reduce the number of footings which would have to be sunk under water Tange devised a system of suspending office blocks between widely spaced towers. The towers would carry lifts and services and were set out on an even grid, some two hundred feet apart. The office blocks were to span between them, cantilevering slightly beyond at the ends. The bottom of some blocks were shown a hundred feet or more above the ground, and they crossed each other at different heights. The great spans were achieved by building the side walls of the offices as triangulated trusses. Space flowed around these elevated office blocks: between, over and under them. While maintaining a high human density Tange produced the promise of an urban environment full of sun, shade, open air and unexpected visual delights.

Tange may never be asked to build his city in Tokyo Bay but the prospects of the suspended blocks continued to fascinate him, and in 1964 he published designs for a concise development of the idea in a single complex building: the Yamanashi Press and Broadcasting Centre at Kofu City. He separated the many activities, put them in private boxes, and spanned them, interspersed at different heights and at right angles to each other, between massive cylindrical service towers. It made the most striking image of the third phase to this date. It had the required ingredients in some strength: simplicity of idea, consistency of structure, yet functional complexity of form; freedom within discipline.

Meanwhile, more ordinary architects with more caution and more modest opportunities all over the world were turning away from the restrictions of the second phase, away from arbitrary modules and symmetry and closed forms. A sense of freedom grew.

Across the Atlantic from Sert, the older Cambridge, and Oxford, neither of which had had any contact with the first or second phases, seemed at last to find their feet in twentieth-century design. The new colleges that arose in the 1960s after these

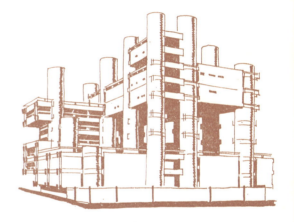

Yamanashi Press Centre

House near Sydney by Ken Woolley

universities finally admitted modern architecture were mostly in the spirit of the third phase; none more so than Cambridge's Churchill College, by Dick Sheppard.

Domestic architecture led the way as usual in more conservative communities. A strong regional branch developed, for instance, in Sydney, where there was a sufficient number of younger architects with enough in common to constitute a school. They abandoned succinct, closed form as they did the glamorous finishes of an earlier phase of Australian Domestic. They preferred over-burnt bricks and naked timber, used inside and outside in the same state. They exploited the steep slopes of the hills around the harbour, sometimes reclining with the slope and sometimes projecting out from it. Enclosed rooms and semi-enclosed spaces in deep recesses, and internal courts open to the sky, and fenced outdoor areas, were all of a kind and interchangeable in a search for a bridge between the primeval gum trees of the sites and the dishwashers in the kitchens.

Across the Pacific some young Californian architects in similar circumstances also were searching for domestic spatial freedom, and along similar lines, though perhaps with more intensity and certainly to the accompaniment of more passionate argument. For a project called 'Sea Ranch', by the ocean a hundred miles north of San Francisco, a partnership of young men led by Charles Moore, the Chairman of Architecture at the University of California at Berkeley—Moore, Lyndon, Turnbull and Whitaker—planned holiday apartments in dense clusters of steeply angled shed roofs, ragged walls and jutting bay windows. The basic unit of space, the general living area for each apartment, was a cube with sides measuring, quite arbitrarily, 24 feet. This repetitive cube was broken into and out of to suit functional variations between apartments. That is, bay windows broke out and subsidiary rooms such as kitchen and bathroom broke in. They were free-standing on their own legs at various levels in the main space. The architects described them as enlarged furniture and referred to 'a four poster bedroom'. Explaining their approach Donlyn Lyndon outlined a philosophy involving the three essential components of the third phase: senses of realism and unity and space. 'We do not reject', he wrote, 'the apparently arbitrary fancies and associations of those for whom we build, but rather seek to fashion from these a sensible order . . . The architect particularizes. He selects an appropriate temperature range . . . controls the intensity and direction of light . . . organizes movement and subjects the building process to a clarifying pattern. By directing all these factors to a controlling image, he builds the opportunity for people to know where they are—in space, in time and in the order of things.'

Although the third phase was quite the latest thing at this time, rather significantly its members did not claim to be doing anything very new. On the contrary, they were quite proud to recognize in much of their work reflections of past glories of early twentieth-century architecture. These reflections were not difficult to find. Frank Lloyd Wright as well as Le Corbusier had built in the spirit of the third phase at some time just as both had built in first or second phases when it suited them. Several of Wright's better known works, like the Johnson Wax Factory, Fallingwater, and many of the prairie houses might be called prototypes of the third phase. Several of his later works, notably two circular buildings finished posthumously, the Church of the Annunciation in Milwaukee, and the Arizona State University's auditorium at Tempe, were clearly decorated monoliths of the second phase. The quality which distinguished the earlier anachronistic examples of third phase was in each case a strong concept based on an idea of function and space rather than on structure or geometry or solid form.

If such a concept is apparent to an observer of any finished building of this century its design may be classed with the third phase, no matter when it was built. This in itself is neither to the credit nor to the discredit of the building. The classification merely throws some light on the intellectual basis of the architectural conception. The validity of the conception and the sense of reality in it determine whether it is successful or not, whether it is good or bad architecture.

I have used the term 'third phase' frankly for convenience in describing the last evolutionary phase of twentieth-century architecture. No doubt many better names could be devised for it. Better still, it should be allowed to return to anonymity. The attachment of some neater or more catchy name might suggest, because of the architectural tradition, that it has a recognizable

Rooms within the room at Sea Ranch

Arizona State University auditorium

155

form. On the contrary it is only a conviction that can lead to a thousand images or guide visions, and thus can have no name in the stylistic sense. Some of its images have suffered already. The random-pylon fashion inadvertently created by Louis Kahn spread fast and subsided predictably. An inconsequential nostalgic device of the Japanese, the habit of crossing the ends of their massive concrete beams in log cabin style, was copied from Scandinavia to South Australia about 1962, then dropped. The fragmentation which Sert so furiously pursued became fashionable in others' hands and thus was doomed. The search for balance, for reality, goes on despite these and other more or less frivolous distractions. The most compelling visual devices of the mid-sixties will lose their fascination and will be replaced by others. Faster and faster. However, nothing is lost provided the convictions are held tight throughout the race and the search for truth proceeds simultaneously.

By the term 'third phase', then, I mean only that after two predictable failures of twentieth-century architecture—first its marriage with the machine and then its search for significant form—at last it seemed to find its feet.

Anybody who is old enough to be reading this has seen in his lifetime a revolution in architecture as great as any of those which gave birth to the Renaissance, the Gothic, the Victorian, or the Functionalist. They have seen the pure white of the International Style scattered as by Newton's prism into a vivid spectrum of different artistic expressions—from the infra-red of Brutalism, as it were, to the ultra-violet of Yamasaki's romanticism. Examination of the better examples all along the range reveals a wealth of intellectual and visual delights, and some architects, impatient with philosophizing, ask can't we be satisfied with these good things, pleased that modern architecture now has as many styles as modern painting; can't we be satisfied with visual pleasures uncomplicated by theory? 'Can't we just wander aimlessly?' as Philip Johnson asked his critics.

If we have any respect for architecture or the human race it houses, we cannot. If anyone doubts this let him look around. The need for an acceptable general philosophy or code of architecture is displayed in nearly every street of the modern industrial world, where a quite calamitous mess swamps the few good or beautiful things made by the better practitioners on the spectrum. Some brilliant men may enjoy themselves and may amuse us greatly while wandering aimlessly, but at their busiest they can do no more than ornament a few peaks rising out of the mess. Some other arts may feel that they can afford not to be bothered with a philosophy. Being free of the need to serve, free of all social obligations and implications, they feel fine and pure. Architecture is never a pure or fine art in this sense. Its great social implications, its influence on all its viewers not to mention its occupiers, its continuous recording of taste, all impede freedom of expression yet immeasurably increase the importance of any expression that does emerge.

Without the social connections architecture is a purer art, a finer art of building follies, a matter of taste or fashion, and at the best an inhibited kind of sculpture.

With the social connections it is less expressive of the individual man and thus less fine or pure as art, but more expressive of mankind and thus indubitably the mother art, the commanding leader of them all. If it has failed to assume this leadership for a century or two, this is not because the other arts have been so strong but because it has been so splintered and divided. If architecture during these last hundred years had had an apparent aim, recognizable and understandable to a reasonable number of people, it would certainly be stronger in itself without necessarily being less enticing or less fun to connoisseurs. Perhaps more importantly it would have tended to carry along towards the same goal the great mass of commercial, industrial, ordinary building which does not pretend to be architecture. It would gradually clear up the mess around its feet. Evidence of this could be found in the record of improving popular design during the short time in which the first phase, or the International Style, held sway.

Just how lacking in mutual aim was the diversified architecture of the second and third phases? Despite the surface differences, clearly the buildings of the various contrary styles had some things in common. At the least they all aimed at staying erect and keeping out the worst of the weather. Was it possible also to find a common denominator of artistic outlook? Was there any quality of good building at which all aimed? A list of nega-

157

tives could be ticked off fairly easily. The mutual aim no longer was simplicity; some of the new work was proudly intricate and deliberately complicated to amuse the eye. And it was not visual beauty. Some, like the Japanese-American Yamasaki, had that aim. Others, like the Japanese-Japanese Tange considered visual beauty something to be reserved for chocolate wrappers or matchbox covers. Although some gentle architects still sought a charming eighteenth-century quality of repose or serenity restated in modern terms, other scorned this in its dead originals and despised it in revival.

Several other well-worn and long-respected terms of artistic merit were no longer approved generally in the 1950s and are not applicable to much design of the sixties. For instance, even the quality of visual unity, once prized above all qualities by every artist and still worshipped by the Monolithicists, has no special attraction or meaning to the many Programmattic Functionalists —or first-phase men—who remain active. Even the word distinction does not fit all, for many new architects try earnestly not to stand out, not to build monuments to themselves, but to blend their buildings politely into whatever surroundings they find themselves in. Then can it be said that modern architecture has nothing in common but the quality of imagination? Not even that, for imagination implies at least a touch of unexpected interest, and Mies van der Rohe, for one, insists that he does not want to be interesting—only good.

Then perhaps goodness, as each sees it, is all that architects of today have in common, but then each sees goodness so differently. In the case of the Mies school, goodness is penetratingly good building in an age of mass-production technology and in a country of steel. To others goodness suggests a more vigorous attack on conventional form to exploit to the full every newest discovery, producing the interesting quality of which Mies is so suspicious.

Nevertheless goodness of structural design is unquestionably one ingredient of all the splinters of serious modern architecture. This is a definable quality, not variable with taste. Whether one is interested in perfecting known techniques or in inventing new ones, there is rarely any difficulty for a trained or experienced builder in discerning immediately at every turn the difference

158

between right and wrong. Rightness lies in obeying the natural laws of statics and of materials. Wrongness lies in disguising materials, misusing or forcing them against their nature.

A similar code may be observed in planning, or the forming and arranging of the various spaces and the overall shape. There has never been a serious architecture that is not disciplined by the functional requirements of the users, and there is not one today. The architect may make mistakes in judgment as to the relationships and the relative importance of various require-ments, and he may sometimes force functions into incorrect, unsuitable spaces—too high or too low, too long or too curved—in order to follow his guide vision. But always he will know the difference between right and wrong in planning, and will only depart knowingly from the former when, under the compulsion of his guide vision, his practical talents fail. But he will know he is wrong. This is not a question of taste.

On the common ground of goodness in structure and correct-ness in planning there grows one other quality which is present in all serious architecture. It is a sense of order. From a Mono-lithic dome to a Brutalist pile of harsh concrete to a hedonistic wrap-around grille, the best new architecture invariably displays, more clearly than many historic styles and in contrast to most other styles since the Early Victorian, a look of inevitability. There is always evidence of a firm step having been taken in the middle stage of the design process, in the conception or formulation of the guide vision. There is evidence of a determination to see the logic of this step carried inexorably through to the last stage of design, down to the smallest details.

Goodness in the structure, correctness for use in the shape, and a sense or order permeating the whole—these qualities are found in all the more celebrated examples of the new architec-tures. It is by no means a coincidence that they also happen to be the qualities which we admire in nature, which are inclined to inspire the poet as well as the most inarticulate tourist with exclamations in praise of a sunset, an ocean, a mountain lake or a stretching cat. They are timeless qualities of good design. They are Functionalist qualities. Whatever the limitations which we can now see so clearly in the early twentieth-century Function-alism, it provided the essential banner necessary to raise the spirits, to hold conviction, and to ensure the single-minded fight to victory over the aesthetic establishment of the time. Yet the early Functionalist theories and practice were usually too gloriously and illogically simple to be convincing for long. The style was too naive and innocent and was readily sidetracked from the principles. The theory of Functionalism got trapped in a white plastered box, and soon became a contentious issue and even an object of ridicule. But form must follow the functions of the users, and the laws of materials and of statics. This should never have become a matter of argument or doubt. It is the only way to a sound architecture. It is the way of the Universe.

To be able to design following the natural laws the architect must know more than the recorded requirements of a plain wall, and a roof in the rain, and a busy client. He must know all the functions and understand fully the implications of them all. He must know all the qualities of the inanimate materials making up the structure, which is comparatively easy, and all the qualities of the human substances being housed, which is impossible. While the architect remains no more than human he will never understand all this. He will therefore never be able to design a fully functional building. Still, he can try. He can, for a start, resist non-functional tendencies. He can select materials which have not been subjected to vulgar abuse in manufacture. He can use what materials are left without pretending that they are anything else. He can resist the seduction of ornament.

In this way his building will have plain materials, used unpretentiously, without ornament—a series of negatives. Early naive Functionalism often was just this: a great negation of bad without being positively good. This was most important at the time, in a positively hideous era, but it was not good enough after the old opposition collapsed. The Functionalist style died not because it was simply functional, as its more insensitive and uncomprehending critics complained, but because it was simply not unfunctional—and was recognized as an ultimately dull, unproductive double negative. Thus the rapid reaction to the positivism of the second phase as soon as the battle was won. Expressionist, Monolithic or Decorated—certainly they were no longer negative, but also often in practice they were a denial of functional principles. Yet there is wide scope for positive action within the functional, natural code of design, and in the third phase architects are busily investigating the possibilities.

For instance, any architect who can acquire a mastery of the medium at his command—all the staple structural methods, all the endless array of composites, plastics and processes, all the engineering principles and the inventions—anyone who masters materials will rise above the structural naïveté that was a part of early Functionalism. He will be able to approach each problem with a touch of Nature's authority. Here is a progressive, hopeful, endless prospect, for science will continue to increase the architect's understanding, and technology will continue to increase his repertoire.

The architect must keep pace with scientific theory and must keep ahead of technology to an extent which enables him to control the latter creatively. If he can do this a fascinating future of infinite structural prospects opens up: a sound materialist Functionalism. For the proper understanding of techniques will eventually put the architect into something like the position of selection and command that Nature enjoys when she designs her branches, leaves, petals, or mountains. It will enable him to design the dog's tail, but still not the dog. It will not assist the architect in a nature-like understanding of the other half of the problem: the real requirements of life, of the human beings that will live in the design or, walking past it, will be moved one way or another by it. To understand these requirements fully the architect must also enjoy a comprehensive understanding of the human material, not just the practical and physiological sides of it, but the psychological, emotional and sentimental sides as well. Only with such understanding will he be able to design in positive and complete Functionalism, as nature does, and thus to create an intellectually and scientifically pure architecture. Since such understanding is impossible, or extremely unlikely for the limited talent of an architect's human brain, one must conclude that pure architecture is unattainable.

A thorough nature-like command of materials may ultimately put half of the architect's creative act, the structural half, on to a scientific basis, but the other half, the human half, appears set to evade intellectual tabulation and command in the foreseeable future. Thus the architectural philosopher reaches a dilemma.

Should the architect do the best possible with the scientific or rational approach, knowing it can take him a long way but never to the end—or should he scrap science and rely on intuition, springing on ahead to any place his imagination will lead him? If he takes the latter course he answers the scientific question with the magic word beauty, and thereafter he allows himself to be led by the emotions, and ultimately he will arrive at buildings which look sublime but have no logical relationship to the realities of the building materials selected, or the life that goes on inside them. After a little contemplation it will be seen that the horns of this philosophical dilemma are labelled Reality and Romance, respectively. Meanwhile, irrespective of philosophy, irrespective of whichever horn is evaded, irrespective of beauty or ugliness, architecture continues behind all argument, inexorably recording society. This is one firm fact which all can accept; it is as evident to you and me contemplating suburbia today as it is to an archeologist piecing together a history from building fragments.

What will any future archeologist make of some of the records of society that we are busy leaving behind us? For instance, an elegant confection of arches, translucent ceilings and lacy screens which he discovers to have been the administration block of a munitions factory? The beauty or ugliness of the building will be of no great interest to him, but he may wonder how sheltered were the lives we led. He may think that the effeminate munitions office block was madly unreal, and that we must have been an evasive race. He may conclude that some of our architects were almost insulting towards our society with the implication of such buildings: that one must falsify realities in order to achieve desirable appearance, or beauty. Yet only a few yards away the future archeologist may discover a strong vigorous utilitarian structure, the factory itself, as honest and unpretentious as the machines that it made, a direct descendant of the first phase of modern architecture. He may then appreciate the heart of the architectural problem in the second half of the twentieth century. It is the question of rational against emotional design, of intellectual against visual beauty, of appropriate against irrelevant images, of reality against romance. It is a moral question because of course the creation of emotional, romantic, irrelevant visions is more amusing and in the short term more rewarding than the rational search for appropriate character, yet the delights of the exercise are gained at the expense of a valid social record and of the experience of reality.

Long before the twentieth century's attempts at realism a division of architecture into romantic and classic schools was recognized, as it is still in most arts, but this is not the important division in architecture now. It is there, and the study of it may be of academic interest, and the meat of some critics, but understanding of it will not help to solve the architectural puzzle. For the romantic and the classic often enough now are mixed in the one building, as in Edward D. Stone's work: classic in form and romantic in detail. The romantic and classic often take the same side in opposition to the realistic. The classic form, in fact, can be romantic in its anti-realism. The very fountainhead of classic form, the noble Parthenon, was romantic, non-realist, in its use of traditional, conventionalized timber structural forms translated into the stone dentils and other ornamental trimmings. In this sense classical architecture wallows in romantic allusions. In these days classicism can be romantic for a different reason. A vision of classic purity, stripped of the dentils to be up-to-date for a mundane modern purpose like a jam factory, may be the most shameless sort of commercial romanticism, giving a spurious dignity to a rather messy function. When the Monaro Mall shopping centre in Canberra is given a lofty arcaded entrance with slender columns raising one's eyes above the price tickets to a glimpse of eternity in a high ceiling of blue—what is there left for the Houses of Parliament?

The puzzle of architecture is not the question of what is beautiful in building, though that may be a fascinating aesthetic question. The real puzzle is in reconciling the undoubted attractions of the merely beautiful to the deep-seated need for a sense of reality in this great servant art. This may be a subconscious need, often enough involving things as close to the heart as the need for security, the fear for the safety of one's shelter in a storm, and the knowledge of its vulnerability to the prowling predators with the mortgage papers.

Building is a serious medium. Anything that is unrealistic and unnecessary weakens its serious purpose, however slightly, and puts some sort of a chink in the protective armour which is the

Monaro Mall

purpose of building. If architecture were not bound to its serious sheltering purpose it would offer no puzzling contradictions. The object would be simply to make it beautiful (by subtly varying the familiar) or exciting (by violently changing it). It would be a delightful decorative art, as often it is now, and nothing more.

The classical form traditions, being unreal today, may look beautiful but cannot make good architecture. This is generally agreed. But sometime, at its very beginning, every persistent classical element was realistic, and not necessarily beautiful. It persisted because it was realistic. Beauty, or familiarity with a touch of the unexpected, grew on to it with maturity. Every part of a building which achieves a sense of realism in its vision, which convinces in its suitability for its purpose, its materials and its moment—every part of a building which achieves a touch of the efficiency of Nature—is likely to command a following. If it is a small thing, like an adjustable louvre, it is likely to create a fashion. If it is a large thing, like the curtain wall, it is likely to create a style. Then its form, as a vision, takes on a life of its own apart from the original. It is dissociated from the real purpose, and becomes no more than a sort of symbol of serious building. It is visually reminiscent and thus sensually satisfying. Thus numerous architectural elements which began life realistically, from the classical column to the tapered *piloti*, are now dissociated from reality, are parts of some style, and are vaguely satisfying to a beholder who knows the style. The style itself may be much more than merely attractive to the casual roving eye of a tourist. It may be truly beautiful to an experienced and sensitive beholder, superb in such visual qualities as pattern, unity, repose. Not shallowly pretty, but evoking responses from deep within one's visual experiences. This kind of beauty can be produced in architecture with as much ease, or difficulty, as it can in any other art. Its production and appreciation can be taught to sensitive people, most effectively by analysis into the designer's techniques of proportion, scale and aesthetic rules such as the golden section, or Hogarth's spiral demonstrating continuity with variety. Examples of such beauty command and deserve the loving attention of historians, critics and students.

Realism and beauty are not, of course, mutually exclusive. Beauty sometimes may be an expression of reality. Sometimes

164

it may be irrelevant; and only the architect, and those who use the building, and those who study it deeply, are likely to know the difference. Irrelevance in no way mars the beauty to all other people, it merely places the work in another category from the realistic.

In short, it can be said that there are two fountainheads of serious building. Out of the great mass of numb practical work and vulgar exhibitionism rise two towers of artistic quality. One is creative, representing the search for reality or building truth. Products of this search are rarely beautiful at first sight, but successes in the search create a new vision. The other is interpretive, representing the translation of this vision, however irrelevantly, into other buildings, as directed by taste and emotion. These are the realist and the romantic sides of architecture.

The twentieth century began with realism, 'the ten-fingered grasp of reality' as Louis Sullivan said. It only drifted into romance about the middle of the century when trying to escape from the glass box. Yet the moral discipline of the first fifty years still lingered on, and produced some bad consciences. Realistic functional reasons were found to justify essentially romantic devices. Sun-shading, for instance, was argued in vindication of the most outrageous external ornamentation in the form of Eastern grilles and curly visors. Confronted with the conflict between realism and romance, only a brave or brilliantly self-confident man today admits to romantic leanings. Even at the height of the second phase the goal of truth was never denied. A generation of architects searched about in all directions, forward and back in time, to East and West, on the erratic wings of intuition, hoping thus to discover reality, or the truth of building. They did not find it. Nor will those who try to reach the truth through realism. But at least the latter look more dignified in the process; and they may get closer. The search for realism can be taken, then, as a starting point in the creation of good architecture.

As well as being an involuntary expression of society's standards and objectives, as well as being useful shelter, architecture has been a personal art which happens to use the medium of space. One must say 'has been' because the future is by no means clear or determined. Prefabrication and other advanced

165

technical processes constantly increase the mechanization of the building operation and coax it away from personal art and lead it more and more towards standardization. At the same time tension, shells, pneumatic and other new structural systems shift the responsibilities little by little from the architect's to the engineer's shoulders. The future could be almost entirely under the control of the mass-production technologist and the engineer, and there are times when the prospects of the architectural profession does not look especially rosy. Yet, despite the harsh words frequently directed towards the impractical and unbusinesslike architect, the world really does want him still. But only if he accepts a slightly changed emphasis that is developing. The balance between artist and scientist in the make-up of the hypothetical architect is being upset. The emphasis is swinging, but not more to the right—the scientific side—as was the rule earlier in the century. It is swinging to the left. In a field now crowded with specialist scientists the architect has to realize that his only justification is to be a better artist. But what kind of artist? Not a creator of monuments to himself, or to irrelevant beauty. He must grow into a humanist, a realist, with sympathy and sensitivity to the requirements of man in all his various shelters.

If a new architecture of meaning, value and consistency is to rise out of the splinters of the first two phases of twentieth-century architecture, it must return to realism. If this can be accepted by the reader, the application of this principle in practice, through the easy stages of design, may now be examined.

Throughout the exercise the realist architect must search his soul and his design at every turn, asking what is realistic and what is unrealistic, what is done only for appearances or by habit or to please the inadequately enlightened taste of his client or the public, what can be eliminated. (If he were romantic, of course, he would be asking no such question of himself. He would proceed by feeling, without reasons, letting beauty, nostalgia, visual drama or excitement guide his hand.)

Realism has a long history in farm buildings, warehouses, experimental scientific laboratories and other utilitarian structures or machines too innocent or busy to think of being romantic. If the same sort of directness or innocence could be retained for the more complex functions of modern life this would be the end of one part of the puzzle. No more could be asked of architectural technique. Unfortunately, sophisticated modern building components such as aluminium window frames, plastics and prestressed panels are not innocent and it is hard to remain innocent when using them. Charles Eames went as far as possible in a well-known house he built for himself among Californian eucalypts. He used stock industrial products straight from the catalogues but assembled them with imagination to prove that pedestrian products need not make a pedestrian building. Still this was not an innocent building. It was extremely sophisticated, though doing its best to look anything but. One cannot recover innocence once it has gone. Realism now must be created consciously step by step.

In the initial stage, the pre-design programming, the realist approach requires a most thorough examination of the human background to the problem, from the viewpoint of the occupier, the neighbour, and society. It required study of rather more than the plain, practical, economical, physical problems as seen by the client, the building inspector and the company's accountant. To answer only these problems is not being realistic, but merely expedient. The architect should be looking further, for the realities of the slice of life that is being housed. Eventually he will attempt to give visual expression to them. He is a sort of portraitist, circumscribed by the conditions of the shelter as if by the character of a sitter. To unearth the realities requires insight, professional skill and experience. No one will lead him to them unsolicited. It is part of his task in writing a programme for the building to decide what the people concerned really need. Any system of commissioning the design of a building which insulates the architect from the users by inserting a committee or other administrative controller may have practical advantages but cannot lead to the finest solutions. This is the fatal flaw in any architectural competition. Here the architect, for obvious reasons, must be restrained from the smallest human contact with the people for whom he is designing. He can never learn intimately what is in the future occupant's mind, not to mention his heart, and is likely to develop the whole concept, like a clever house of cards, without a foundation. For the same reason a speculative investment building can never be the most sensitive exposition of the

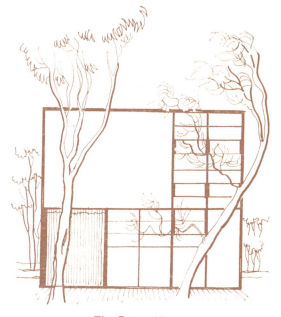

The Eames House

architectural art. This is not to deny that the modern tendency is towards anonymous clients—that is, buildings designed for investors, developers, committees and commissions. Such clients may encourage a perfection of organization and technology, but they also lead to anonymous architecture.

However, while the old humane art of architecture lasts there is much enjoyment to be had from its portraiture of human activities. The realist architect in the meantime must recognize that a human being is not simply a lump of flesh to be kept dry at a temperature range between sixty-eight and seventy-five degrees. These real and special lumps have other properties, such as minds that get strong illusions about their own importance, and beliefs about God, and feelings about space; certain longings, to be free and unfenced, or to be back in the womb. It is part of the function of a building to pander to these needs, and illusions of needs.

Yet this is a danger point in the philosophy of architectural realism. For a stretch of the meaning of functional design to include psychological coddling of the occupants can be taken as licence to include any arbitrary shallow shape or decorative device. The most outrageous Gothic Revivalist or Contemporary interior decorator has never admitted to lack of necessity for his most frenzied fretwork or violently-coloured Mondrianesque checkerboards. Ornament, they say, is useful and necessary; it soothes the tired businessman or it satisfies his wife's love of pretty things. But if in the act of placating the savage human ornament is unrealistic in relation to the building structure, then it is a primitive deception not compatible with a civilized community's self-respect.

A balanced realism requires a sensitive respect for all matter 'as found', to use the Brutalists' phrase. Balance is essential; it is unrealistic to build a Gothic church today, for obvious economic and structural reasons; there is no more argument on that. Yet it would not be realistic to deny that numerous nice people feel closer to God in Gothicky surroundings. It would be unrealistic to deny the influence of centuries of associations of this kind, and to build a church with a ceiling height of eight feet. Yet there is clearly a difference between sympathy with genuine human passions in aesthetics, however absurd, and the exploitation of

168

human weaknesses. An architect need not forsake the realist cause in admitting sympathy and understanding for another human's frailties. He can still analyse realistically the other's activities, needs, and aspirations. Those needs, however unreal they may appear to the architect, seem real to their holder, and can be answered realistically. It is possible for instance to build a realistic building for an unrealistic function, such as a meeting house for some weird religious sect. It would be realistic to consider the theatrical qualities of the service and to provide the means for drawing out the drama. It would be realistic to consider the importance to the individual of being consciously one of many in the act of worship, and to design an interior which accentuated the common cause of the gathering. It would be realistic to consider the dignity and faith of the worshipper despite his belonging to this weird sect with which one can have no patience. Yet religious architecture, even for ordinary, respectable sects, even by respected architects working nominally in the modern idiom, customarily contains so much that is unreal as to remove it from the company of serious architecture. It is not realistic, for example, to shape the roof of a church in the form of a pair of hands, finger tips touching in the traditional pose of prayer. Yet this is what Frank Lloyd Wright, no less, was proud to admit as the inspiration of his guide vision for the well-known Unitarian church near his home in Madison, Wisconsin. This is abstract-symbolic sculpture with no bearing on the realities of the act of congregating or the emotions of worship.

Realism in any building must be based on a sympathetic analysis of the real needs of the occupants. There is general agreement now that a realistic bank is not one with Roman columns on the front to impress customers with its permanence and invulnerability; there is no more argument on the use of columns. Yet a bank is no more realistic if it adopts an excessive gaiety of glass and random colours suggesting openhandedness and a generous liberal outlook, designed to counter a tendency in the opposite direction in the overdraft department. A bank, as an office, should be open, light and sterile; perhaps more transparently honest than most offices, to reassure the customer. But no more than that. It is not a dress salon nor an espresso bar. Yet they too have their own realities.

Realism in architecture means dealing with humans as they are, and with their activities as they are, but not with their shallow visual tastes: with their habits but not their beliefs. It calls for radical changes in artistic character from case to case: for appropriateness in character to fit each case. Yet Mies van der Rohe, who is hardly an unrealistic man, exercised his great influence after World War II in the contrary direction. He taught and demonstrated, in effect, realism to technology, and let appropriate character take care of itself in the artefacts, icons and gewgaws with which people will inevitably surround themselves. This was a prophetic and almost cynical variation on the theme of realism, rather than a contradiction of it. Undoubtedly there will come a time when the realities of building technology, of mass-production and prefabrication, will be so compelling as to overrule the demands for individuality. Then the doctrine of realism will demand an end to appropriateness of character in the design of individual buildings. But that time is still far away. Until technology eclipses the art of individual building a strong statement of appropriate character is not only possible, it is the only justification for the continuance of the partly obsolete profession of architecture. A magnificent, cosmic beauty and repose may one day reside in the technologist's enclosure of space, but even the most beautiful and universal technological enclosure cannot have individual character. It cannot stimulate for long, or make one more aware of human values, or heighten the experience of any phase of life. Only individual designs can do these things, and should, until the time comes for the artists of architecture to step aside and leave all construction to the technologists. That time need not be hastened unduly.

In the meantime appropriate character is called for. Appropriateness in architecture last century meant aptness of the selected historical style: Gothic for churches, Scottish Baronial for the new knights, and so on. Most of these style associations are considered laughable nowadays, but the practice continues in more whimsical or sophisticated ways. Voluptuous arcades, excessively slender and lofty columns, excitingly curved vaults and reverently pointed roofs, and so on, are used for atmospherics. They cannot be accused of revivalism, for nothing but the associations are being revived. They are merely snippets, quotations from the classics, out of context, but reminiscent and evocative enough to pass for architectural statements. Even outright revivalism could hardly be less real than this dressing up, this staging of theatrical effects. Real architecture cannot rely on allusions. Realist architectural character must necessarily create rather than borrow or steal. Character implies in a building, as in a man, integrity, wholeness, an entity directed to an end. It demands the old artistic quality of unity, intensity and singleness of idea throughout the design; for two sources of motivation in a building, as in a man, do not double the value of one source, but halve it.

A single motivation means a single idea, in artistic terms a single image, to be followed through against all counter attractions and counter claims during the process of design and construction, a formal order in which a rightness of structure and planning are combined. In short, a strong guide vision. Without this there can be no sense of wholeness in the building. Thus there can be no strong character nor coherent expression.

Now, there is something odd about this all-important stage of design: the conception of a guide vision. It does not really require an architect—that is, anyone with an architect's training and experience. It demands a capacity for summing up a problem, for extracting the heart of it and for inventiveness to solve it, a capacity for ridding the mind of inhibiting precedents. It demands an innocent ability to jump to conclusions. All these are different qualities from those reasonably associated with the person of a successful architect.

The professional architect in his dark grey suit needs a tidy mind and a human understanding to sort out, during the first stage of design, a concise programme from the tangled set of requirements. He also needs a special sort of capacity for visual orderliness, to see him through the final stage of the design process when the guide vision is developed into a real building. Various other qualities are also helpful, such as a head for figures and a good cocktail manner, not to mention fortitude during the more demanding phases of administration in the course of running the actual building contract. All these admirable qualities, essential to a complete professional, are not the kind of qualities traditionally associated with sensitive evocation of ideas and images. The surprising thing is that the two kinds of capacity do sometimes coincide in one man, if only very rarely. Usually an architect acknowledges his comparative weakness on one side or the other and bolsters this side with hired assistants. A most unusual thing about the practice of architecture is that it is divisible. This is what makes it humanly possible: more than one can play. But only one can evoke the vision.

Some of the strongest architectural or constructional images in the modern world were created by others than architects. Paxton's great vision which produced the epochal Crystal Palace of 1851 was based on structure and a bright idea or dream of a giant glasshouse. Nervi's images of great domes spun on rib skeletons of Gothic elegance, Candela's images of tortured planes locked in equilibrium, and Fuller's images of geodesic domes to cover whole cities, are all engineers' visions. From them came some of the most important, most copied, architectural spaces of this half of the twentieth century. But Nervi and Candela and Fuller do not pretend to be architects, and presume to design only spaces which serve the greatest but simplest of functions: sheltering masses of people, or things. They leave the 'architecture', planning the entrances, conveniences and partitions, to architects. Nevertheless these big three, as well as some other engineers, have the visionary quality necessary to create architecture. Plenty of other people have it: some sculptors, art directors of films, stage designers, and many others whose creative faculties are visually biased. This visionary ability cannot very well be taught, although it can be cultivated. Almost anyone who wants to develop it is likely to succeed; it is not magical or exceptionally rare. The reason for so much bad building is not the absence of visions but the absence of the experience and capacity needed to curb them, control them, and eliminate the meaningless ones. The sculptor's or the stage designer's vision will always exceed the architect's in visual brilliance, as the engineer's will in structural ingenuity.

The architect's problem as he stirs the puzzle pieces and searches inside himself is to evoke a vision that has something of the visual quality of a sculptor's vision, as much as possible of the structural purity of the engineer's vision, and as well an arrangement of spaces that will serve and satisfy or stimulate

172

its users. To evoke such a vision he needs a strong three-dimensional creative sense, of course, but even before this he requires analytical and editorial ability to draw out the full and vital programme of requirements on which to base the vision. In the case of the more intimately human shelters such as houses and hospitals his understanding of human needs should extend to a compassion that will enable him to see a great deal beyond the merely physical and economic demands.

We can picture, then, a paragon of an architectural artist. He will be a sensitive, sympathetic investigator of human needs, patient enough to assemble a complete set of puzzle pieces, the insistent but inconsistent demands of the users, before he begins to fit any of them together. He will have that visionary quality that enables him to free his mind of irrelevant precedents and to jump to an apt, concise resolution of all the puzzle pieces. He will have the visual imagination to see his solution in terms of form and spaces. He will also have the sensitivity to three-dimensional detail to preserve that image through the long process of design until the last recalcitrant sewer pipe has been tucked into its niche in the pattern.

Such a hypothetical paragon could be the messiah in a creative-realistic philosophy of the art. Few real men are able to muster anything like the required number of talents, let alone the ability as well to carry on after design is finished in the second, equally demanding half of the architect's work: the administration of the economics of the building operation. Nevertheless, no matter how far perfection is out of the reach of the ordinary human architect, a philosophy or concept of perfection still has practical advantages for him. It sets up a yardstick, not just for judging other architects' designs, which offers few difficulties, but for judging his own, for judging every move he makes in achieving his own design.

There is a series of three questions he may ask himself at every crucial step in the design process. Working back from finished solution to the puzzle pieces, these questions are: first, is it an orderly, whole, indivisible thing? One may put this question another way and ask: has it character? If the answer to this is negative there is hardly need to pursue the matter. If affirmative, the second question concerns the nature of the character. Is it meaningful, appropriate, heightening the experience of the human activity being housed; is it creative, rather than nostalgic or borrowed or stolen? And if it seems to pass this test also, then finally: is the character achieved validly, by assembling the pieces of the puzzle and not by means of adding irrelevant new pieces or by sweeping some of the more inconvenient ones off the table?

Knowing that such questions will be asked, if not by others then at least by himself, puts a necessary discipline on the architect. To try to achieve an affirmative answer to the first test, of character, he will be more vigilant in his avoidance of all extraneous, character-weakening elements. He must, at the start, take a firm stand on the matter of ornament and decorative devices. He will need all his strength to shun them. This matter gives difficulty to some good people. It constitutes for them a major puzzle of architecture, for it must be recognized that few serious philosophies of architecture throughout history make anything but apologies for decoration, yet at the same time one has to recognize a human weakness for ornaments. Civilization implies the disappearance of ornament from the object of use, Adolf Loos declared, and one generation agreed with him, but with the next generation ornament came creeping back. And many argued: why not? How ridiculously puritan was the Loos posture! If ornament is enjoyed for aesthetic or sentimental reasons, who should be permitted to discredit it, let alone ban it? Louis Sullivan wrote once: 'It is not evident to me that ornament can intrinsically heighten [architecture's] elemental qualities.' Yet he himself was the most delightful and shameless decorator of thoroughly self-sufficient designs. Ornament was like a drug with him, or a love affair in public, but his flamboyant, meaningless, lovingly detailed doodling had little or nothing to do with his architecture.

At the height of the Functionalist influence a person's level of aesthetic education and taste could be measured by inverse proportion to the number of ornaments in his home. Yet even the most ascetic recluse was likely to harbour just one or two little pieces somewhere, retained for some personal meaning probably not apparent to anyone else. Such pieces are of course different again from the craftsman's kind of ornament.

Both the craftsman's ornament and the collector's ornament can be respected without allowing architecture the licence which

Sullivan ornament

174

Loos withdrew. The serious architect has to deny himself the comforting excuse that ornament can have a public psychological function. It does have some psychological value, of course, but mainly to the architect himself, to him who designs or carves it. It also may have some value to him who regards it as some sort of keepsake, and an architect's ornament may gather to itself in time a keepsake value. Sullivan's, Wright's and Griffin's have done this, but not because of their own value, only because in time their ornament drew a meaning from the strong buildings with which it was associated. Ornament is essentially parasitic. The more strength it draws to itself the weaker grows the body of its host. When new, before any keepsake value can be attached to it, any architect's ornament is a poor thing with no meaning except perhaps a spurious one of association with other buildings. It can only weaken the wholeness and the realness of the building.

After the counter-revolution of the 1950s and its overthrow of the Loos discipline, when ornament returned to modern architecture, it appeared at first in comparatively restrained forms in the work of Yamasaki, Stone and the Italians. Then it flowed in uninhibited profusion on to the work of numerous lesser men. To most responsible architects ornament remained at best highly suspect. Often it seemed positively degrading to the spirit of architecture. There was always, however, one source of ornament that remained respectable. This was the invited work of art: the mural or the fresco, the sculpture stuck above the entrance door. In all honesty this was still ornament as surely as if it had been cast to an architect's scale drawing, but it escaped the stigma by being called art. It was done by an artist instead of a paper-hanger, or by a sculptor instead of a blacksmith, but still it was ornament—rich man's, culvitated man's, ornament. Artists and sculptors could always be found who would accept the task of filling in holes in the architect's design. Frequently they had nothing but scorn for the working mother art, but imagined they could rescue something from the impossible situation by developing some expressive theme of their own, independent and proudly irrelevant. Others have tried to absorb an architectural theme into their own medium. Either way the artist is certain to do less than his best work on a free canvas.

175

The architecture-art affair is historically unsuccessful, from the Sistine Chapel to Coventry Cathedral. This is not to suggest that any marriage between architecture and another art without injury to either is impossible. But a love match between cultivated grown-up individuals is rather different from a marriage arranged by the parents in accordance with tribal custom before either character is formed.

Our paragon, the creative-realist architect, should have—like any other civilized man, it is to be hoped—a proper and sensitive respect for the work of his brothers in the arts of painting and sculpture. If he does, he will not dream of asking them to help him out of holes in the architectural design. He will complete the building without blanks or apologies. Then perhaps if someone wishes to introduce a painting or a sculpture, or a choir, he will welcome these for their own value, but not in the hope that they will blend with or will bolster his architecture. Painting had difficulties enough trying to mate with architecture in Michelangelo's day, and then both were under comparable disciplines. Now that the discipline of realism has tightened around architecture, while all disciplines have been slashed away from painting and sculpture, the marriage is usually a shotgun affair between incompatibles. There can be nothing much more incongruous and ridiculing to all concerned than a huddle of junk sculpture or a slash and dribble of abstract painting carefully built in to a precision-made wall with a primly detailed aluminium trim around it trying to act as a wedding ring.

The object of the architect during the final, detailed stage of the design process is to develop into realization a complete building scheme while holding intact the imaginative statement that was contained in essence in the vision. The vision is his guide and discipline. It is too late now for new or better ideas. There will be numerous counter-influences and side-attractions likely to divert the developing design from realization of the vision. The architect needs all his concentration and integrity to ignore them. Ornament can be regarded as one of the least subtle of these threats. It is like an over-handsome, plausible bounder, but one too obvious in his seductive ways to offer the most serious threat to innocent building. Sheer trickery is more dangerous. In the course of development of all but the simplest designs there comes a time when some practical consideration conflicts with the vision. This may be in a part of the plan; perhaps a necessary stair that will not fit in with the vision no matter how it is turned around, elongated, or squeezed up. It may be a part of the structure, perhaps the shape of a concrete roof, where best engineering principles and the spirit of the vision cannot be made to coincide. Each time the architect is faced with a moral choice. If the inconsistent element is small enough and the vision is strong enough to carry it, for example that rear stair at Ronchamp, the architect will usually accept the inconsistency and be honest about it. If the inconsistency is so great that such honesty is likely to shatter the vision, the architect may decide to reject the vision. He may realize that the recalcitrant stair or the engineering facts of the roof shell should have been among the original puzzle pieces. He may admit to himself that his vision would have been different if he had but known these real conditions at the time of conception. He may start again. But, even if he wants to do this, only rarely do the conditions of professional practice permit him to retrace his steps. By the time he learns of the inconsistencies he is usually fully committed to the vision, for his clients and their money are already deeply involved with it. Thus with human weakness the architect tries to make the best of the inconsistent item. In point of fact there are at his disposal many methods of protecting the vision against these practical assaults on it. A reluctant stair in an office building, for instance, may be pressed into invisible submission by enclosing it with dark glass and horizontal strips at every floor level just the same as the office space alongside—a thorough disguise that will never be detected from the outside by an admirer of the building. Or the structural difficulty can be overcome by not building the roof in shell concrete after all, but by making it in the conventional way with beams and ribs, and then covering all these over with a separate roof and a neat flush ceiling. And again no outside observer will ever know the difference. But in so disguising the truth of the plan or the structure the architect will have destroyed the reality of the building, reduced its ability to represent the overall nature of the activity it houses, and reduced its power to heighten the experience of that activity by its users.

In the final detailed stage of design the social and scientific

177

responsibilities of the architect's work in recording civilization come closest to the surface. Acceptable behaviour can be defined, as it cannot be in either the programming or visualizing stages. Individual differences of architectural technique show up as each inconsistency is solved one way or the other. Ornament, and confidence-trickery in hiding facts of plan and structure, are unacceptable not for moral theoretical reasons but because they affront the reality, and the art of architecture is nothing if not an expression of reality. If any architect believes it is a matter of pure visual delight, he would serve society better as a window-dresser. Nevertheless the architect needs a mastery of visual rules to be able to control and express the reality. He must know the academic code of design: scale, symmetry and assymmetry, optical corrections, balance, and compositional devices of many kinds. Some people know these instinctively, and if not there are textbooks galore to teach them, and the dullest student can learn them. What the dullest student sometimes fails to learn is that these devices are of little value for their own sake outside a shop-window or a stage-setting. They are valuable only inasmuch as they are used to point up the reality of the building.

For instance, the most essential Victorian rule of composition called for a centre of interest, to which the poor roving eye, exhausted by so many carvings and cornices, could gravitate and find rest. Such a point often was a handsomely enriched portico. Eyes were drawn to it inevitably by the rules of perspective, massing and symmetry. It stood four-square beneath the tower, just where the cloisters' converging lines pointed. If in fact this portico held the main entrance to the building one was fortunate, but if the real entrance happened to be elsewhere, the portico still had to be placed at the focal point, 'for architectural reasons', as they said, and a new subsidiary entrance would be driven through at this point to justify the portico. Our false devices today are more sophisticated and the architect needs constant vigilance to keep his own work directed to the ultimate aim of forthright construction.

The hardest task of all is escaping the perverting influence of fashion. The nineteenth century, although full of styles, was conservative and slow in response to fashions. The twentieth century has in the historical sense only one manner, which we call modern, but it changes fashions, as we have seen, as often and as inconsistently as the world of dress design. For style relates to the serious matters of design, to one's philosophy and background, to a building's place in society, while fashion relates to the frivolous side, to shapes and colours and the use or disuse of ornament. The principal guide visions of this century are not at heart as different from each other as all are different from the styles of any previous century. Each fashion, as it has arrived, has temporarily captured the vision of the century, and has more or less deluded and corrupted its architects. This comment does not apply to most who are strong and consistent enough in their views to create a fashionable vision. Wright did not change. Le Corbusier does not change. Mies does not change. But one day Mies is king and the next day he is deposed and Louis Kahn sits there. The only rule is the visual one which also controls the length of skirts and the cut of necklines: the pendulum rule. Levitation of buildings is done, then overdone, then overthrown, and buildings suddenly plummet to the ground and are staked there by heavy pylons. Once lightness was everything; now the rule is massiveness. Yesterday colour was black and white. Today it is a full spectrum. Tomorrow it will be black and white again. The object of the creative architect is to climb above the numbing limitations of the fashions—to use colour, for instance, not for its own attractive value, but to enhance and project his architectural vision.

The path to truth or realism is made more difficult by the technologist who devises better and better deceits on materials to sell products for the building-component manufactures. The crafty deceits of last century, such as 'graining' or 'marbling' done on humble wood or plaster by a simple painter with a crude comb, offered no serious threat to realism. They were always something of a joke, an inept conjurer's trick which tricked no one although it vaguely entertained all. The twentieth century's tricks, such as colour-photographed wood and marble grains reproduced faultlessly on laminated plastic sheets, are a different kind of performance. They are meant to trick people, and they usually succeed. A plastic table top is not only proof to scratches, cigarette burns and stains of ink or claret, in addition it can actually look like a fine, warm-grained piece of timber. Not better

179

than timber. The manufacturers are subtle enough to realize that an occasional imperfection in the smooth grain increases the illusion. This alcohol-proof surface, so much more practical and labour-saving than timber, has also the cosy, reassuringly natural look, reminding the user of the great primitive world beyond the air-conditioning. The technologist's understandable human tendency is to make himself better loved by such clever deceits. Eventually, in the years after architecture has passed away, he will give humanity complete push-button control of his surroundings. Not merely air-conditioning with atmospheric scents, but total artificial environment, a grand extension of the principle of back-screen projection. Imagine the happy home-owner in an enclosed cellar of the future. The silent air-conditioning is restrained from being too perfect by deliberate injections of a barely perceptible draft at random intervals to simulate natural breezes. The walls and ceiling merge in a continuous surface made of some sort of cloudy white blanket material. A control panel near the right hand of the master of the house produces on this continuous surface flickerless moving images in full colour and three dimensions of any of a number of pre-selected and pre-recorded environments: a country glade, a beach, a mountain top (summer view standard; autumn optional extra), a cave, a sitting-room of Buckingham Palace, the White House garden. Faint scent and sound effects complete a total delusion of the senses. Such superb unreality may make architecture finally and completely obsolete for everyday use. But then, perhaps, the very ability to create total beautiful unreality may make some nonconformists, trouble-makers, more appreciative of imperfect reality in building when they can discover it. So in that distant future there may be little esoteric groups of architecture lovers, like philatelists, meeting privately in rooms of stripped concrete. Meanwhile we should keep in mind that every technological advance which ingratiates itself by a rustic twist is leading us closer to the ultimate artificiality of canned environment.

To pass the second test, on the appropriate nature of the character, the realist architect will examine more sharply the character of his vision and ask himself if he is not deluded in his love for it. Is not its attraction after all no more than its ability to remind one of previous architectural delights? He must insist on character being original. This is not the same thing as seeking newness or novelty for its own sake. But satisfaction with the pleasures of visual memory holds us back in a jungle of sentiment. To escape the accelerating race of fashions it is necessary to revise our attitude to architectural character, to reject the notion that rational, realist, functional design represents one stock atmospheric type in building; to break our habit of confusing technique with character, and identifying certain characters with different regions and different architects. Realist-functional design is indeed doomed if it is taken as some sort of a substitute for a human architect, if architects believe that any set of rules can provide with mathematical precision the idea behind the building. There is, we all know, no substitute for creative thought. But realist-functional design, in ever stricter interpretation, with ever firmer denunciation of applied aids, can and must provide the discipline under which the architect's idea is worked out to its conclusion in terms of building materials.

We must be strict. A liberal interpretation of the meaning of realism destroys the concept altogether. It has never been unusual for an architect to imagine that he is serving purpose and reality with the greatest possible economy. Only the purpose has varied from age to age. Early this century the definition of a building's function was finally narrowed down to the purely physical requirements of the occupants, and a new discipline tightened about this wonderfully solid, universal standard. But in its recent state of vacillation, architecture stretched the definition again and allowed what were called 'psychological functions'. It might as well have sanctioned 'symbolic functions' or 'romantic functions', or 'advertising functions'—in short, anything that suited any mean mercenary purpose.

Dissatisfied with the monotony of the first phase of Functionalist architecture, with the 'inhuman' mechanized boxes, disappointed to find so few monumental qualities, so few symbols, such numb response to any call to the spirit, architects turned in the second phase against the principles which once promised to remake the world of design. They did not dream of searching in themselves to find why their ideas were so thin that they let down the principle. But the fundamental weakness was in the low quality and lack of variety of architectural ideas.

What matters is the strength of the vision—or of what remains of it after it is fully developed. What matters to the spirit of realism is whether the requirements of purpose are misinterpreted or distorted, or are in any way not suitably served by the vision when developed without stress or embellishment. What matters to the spirit of realistic creation is whether or not the result is at ease within the laws of nature, of structure, of materials. What matters in terms of art is whether the vision is developed consistently enough to permeate the entire work. And what matters to the spirit of architecture is the extent to which the development of the vision exploits the qualities of space and enclosure.

These, however, are merely rules of technique and style—not of character, which cannot recognize rules or limitations. The essence of character is in the originating vision. If the first phase of twentieth-century architecture was monotonous, this was only because the pioneers had so much work to do in creating and establishing a revolutionary technique that they hardly had time to encourage spatial visions. Any ideas they had were confined within a narrow range. Structure was approved as a stimulus by the unwritten architectural rules of the time. Visions based on wide spans or cantilevers were always well accepted, but visions based simply on the enjoyment of living, or springing from a sense of humour, or gaiety, or reverence, or mystery, or awe, were suspect, because they could not be bound into a specification. They worried the Functionalists, who wondered if such visions could be functional. Questions of function and reality should never have been confused with visions. The place for realism is at the beginning, in the formulation of the programme. The place for Functionalism is the final, detailed development of the image into a complete building design. But the middle, major act of design cannot be bound by either discipline. It is the place for free visions.

If buildings often are too restlessly inconsistent and undirected, it is because the restraints of realism are lifted from the earliest stage and the discipline of Functionalism is removed from the final stage. Thus architects seek visions in regions beyond the scope of the puzzle pieces, and develop these visions with the help of devices which are unworthy of the mother art.

182

At the outset, before design begins, the realist architect collects every material and human fact of relevance to the project, setting himself a puzzle to reconcile them. In the major act of design the creative architect solves this puzzle by a vision of form, which states the reconciliation in architecture's terms of occupied space. In the process of detailed design the Realist-functionalist returns to protect the vision, to strengthen and develop it while observing the integrity of materials and the logic of planning.

Since the principal material fact of relevance to every project is its construction, no one can consider himself an architect unless he has by nature, or until he acquires by experience, a feeling of authority over construction. This means a broad command of the mathematics and technologies and knacks euphemistically known nowadays as Building Science. It means thinking first in structural terms. Again, since the basis of all design is order, no building can be considered architecture unless all its parts are disciplined by some intrinsic system, or pattern of being. But even after all that the building may be no more than an object, a thing in the nature of any industrial product, like a well-designed electric jug or a fine piece of pottery. For it to come alive as a model of the mother art the essential creative step of design must ensure that the building science and the structural scheme are directed to the making of notable (if not always transcendental) spaces, and the intrinsic order of the planning is based on realities of living.

The two most insistent and persistent qualities of architectural design may always remain conflicting: on the one hand, a morality based on reflections of the truth of construction and a valid image of society in its shelter; on the other, the lure of beauty— always personal, often irrelevant. But despite the ambivalent nature of the art, the design process does allow for a consistent philosophy or working code. The central creative step permits the artistic freedom which individual designers must enjoy if architecture is to live, while the ethics and disciplines of technological-functional design are maintained in the first and last steps. An understanding of this division builds some foundation for criticism of others' and one's own work, and permits one to hope for a future in which idealism and realism are not in conflict but are equally balanced and mutually respected.

Now for the benefit of any reader who, quite understandably, is impatient enough to seek prematurely the last paragraphs to find out if, or how, the author has tried to present any resolution to the enigma, here for what it is worth is my concluding attempt to answer the central puzzle.

It may be stated thus: after the physical and practical problems are solved, what is the architect trying to do?

It may be answered thus: a perfect piece of architecture would solve all the functional problems with one decisive and appropriate concord of spaces. Yet there are two difficulties here. As ordinary mortals architects cannot ever know all the functional problems, and as practical men they are only rarely free to explore the range of spatial experiences. Therefore perfect architecture is impossible. But architects can aspire to it by being realistic in facing the problems they do know, by shunning irrelevancies, and by exploring the delights of defined space as far as each problem permits.

INDEX